The Servant Leader and High School Change

More Lessons from Principal to Principal

Rocky Wallace

ROWMAN & LITTLEFIELD EDUCATION
Lanham • New York • Toronto • Plymouth, UK

OTHER BOOKS IN THIS SERIES

Principal to Principal: Conversations in Servant Leadership and School Transformation

Published in the United States of America
by Rowman & Littlefield Education
A Division of Rowman & Littlefield Publishers, Inc.
A wholly owned subsidiary of The Rowman & Littlefield Publishing Group, Inc.
4501 Forbes Boulevard, Suite 200, Lanham, Maryland 20706
www.rowmaneducation.com

Estover Road
Plymouth PL6 7PY
United Kingdom

Copyright © 2009 by Rocky Wallace

All rights reserved. No part of this publication may be reproduced, stored in a retrieval system, or transmitted in any form or by any means, electronic, mechanical, photocopying, recording, or otherwise, without the prior permission of the publisher.

British Library Cataloguing in Publication Information Available

Library of Congress Cataloging-in-Publication Data
Wallace, Rocky, 1956-
 The servant leader and high school change : more lessons from
    principal to principal / Rocky Wallace.
   p. cm.
 Includes bibliographical references and index.
 ISBN-13: 978-1-57886-951-0 (hardcover : alk. paper)
 ISBN-13: 978-1-57886-952-7 (pbk. : alk. paper)
 ISBN-13: 978-1-57886-953-4 (electronic : alk. paper)
 ISBN-10: 1-57886-951-X (hardcover : alk. paper)
 [etc.]
 1. High schools—United States—Administration. 2. High school principals—United States. 3. Educational change—United States. I. Title.
 LB2822.2.W35 2009
 373.1200973—dc22   2008041481

∞ ™ The paper used in this publication meets the minimum requirements of American National Standard for Information Sciences—Permanence of Paper for Printed Library Materials, ANSI/NISO Z39.48-1992
Manufactured in the United States of America.

This book is dedicated to all the many mentors who have blessed me over the years by taking the time to share their insights, and more importantly, model for me true servant leadership. And at the top of the list are Mom and Dad, who gave up personal dreams to follow the call into ministry and to put their five children through college. They stayed focused on their faith, vision, and purpose. And today, in so many different ways, they see their work now reaching into the future through the lives of their children, children through marriage, and their twelve grandchildren. Mom and Dad's model for living well never has been about worldly success. Instead, their model is far more priceless because it remains centered, after all these years, on timeless principles of goodness and the loving support of others who are placed in their lives. Yes, they are mentors. My first mentors. And I love them more than I can say.

Contents

Preface		vii
Acknowledgments		ix
1	Time	1
2	Calendar Management	5
3	Priorities	9
4	Integrity Heals the Culture	13
5	"Barnyard" Politics	17
6	Instructional Support	21
7	Students Know What Is Missing	25
8	Holding Teachers Accountable	29
9	Abusers of Children	33
10	Jocks	37
11	Peer Harassment (The Unspoken Subculture)	41
12	Modeling—Leading by Doing	47
13	Hiring the Best	51
14	Seniors—Prepared for Life?	55

15	Curriculum—If Not Relevant, It Is Useless	61
16	"Puppy Love" or Obsession?	67
17	Cheerleaders	73
18	Narcissism	77
19	Termination—Calling the Terrorist's Bluff	83
20	Serving	89
21	Core Values Drive Everything!	95
22	Passage	99
23	Mentor	103
24	Leadership Cadres	109
25	Closing Thoughts	115
References		119
About the Author		121

Preface

In working with educators every day who are down in the trenches making a difference in the lives of their students, I have come to realize something that is so, so exciting. We already have in place the talent and resources to transform our educational system in the United States. The problem is not lack of knowing how to develop our children and youth so they indeed reach their full potential. The problem, as with many complex organizations, is that significant parts of the system are broken. Thus, in many schools, a toxic culture exists—a culture that fosters built-in barriers to learning.

No, it's not that these schools are not working hard and producing impressive results in some key areas year after year. But when compared to their potential, they are not what can be called great schools. The numbers do not lie. Across our nation, high school students still drop out of school at some point along the way in alarming numbers. And the majority of those who do make it to graduation day do not go on to complete college or other postsecondary training. Yes, the *majority*. Hence, bottom line: We have a scarcity of truly great schools. Some would argue that we have a scarcity of what could even be called good schools (if we are measuring effectiveness with cumulative student potential).

This book, as a follow up to *Principal to Principal: Conversations in Servant Leadership and School Transformation*, tells the story of a burned out high school principal who has multiple careless leadership issues. But with the help of a mentor who understands the potential of any school to rise out of the ashes of mediocrity, surprising changes begin to take place at Blue Creek High School. Not new, "fix it" programs that cost thousands of dollars. Not the continuance of the catering to the few at the expense of the many. But instead a transformation of the *entire* community, beginning with one man who finally understands what it means to be a servant leader.

Acknowledgments

I am so thankful to have crossed paths with Dr. Tom Koerner and Rowman & Littlefield Publishers. Our partnership has been a joy, and the Rowman & Littlefield staff who assist me are wonderful examples of servant leadership.

The educational organizations I have had the opportunity to work with over the years continue to inspire me with their good and faithful work in making a difference in the lives of students of all ages. To the staff at Fallsburg School in Lawrence County, Kentucky, thank you for being so supportive of a new principal back in 1991. I experienced a true community school at Fallsburg, one of the best kept secrets in eastern Kentucky.

And Catlettsburg Elementary, thank you for allowing me to serve you as you taught me so, so much about how "blue collar" schools can shoot for the stars and do amazing things when willing to not settle for just being a "good" school.

While serving at the Kentucky Department of Education (KDE) as a mentor to new principals, a fellow former principal who became a mentor himself to me was David Simpson. Dave is still at KDE, sharing his insights with school leaders across Kentucky.

Perhaps one of the most rewarding experiences I have ever been a part of was working with our field staff in adult education while at the Kentucky Educational Development Corporation in Ashland, Kentucky. Adult education often flies beneath the radar, but plays such a vital role in assisting adults of all ages in getting refocused on education and going on to attain a college degree and other post-secondary training.

My professors and colleagues at Regent University's School of Global Leadership and Entrepreneurship continue to do cutting edge work in preparing today's leaders for a world of constant change. My training at Regent continues to be invaluable to me in my writing and in teaching servant leadership principles to graduate students.

To my colleagues and students at Morehead State University, you inspire me daily with your commitment to changing lives by opening minds and opening doors to so much more to those who will just take that first step.

And I would be remiss if I did not thank Calvary Christian School for allowing me to stop in a couple of early mornings a week to teach PE classes. Calvary staff, I love your formula for how to educate the "whole" child. You are making a huge, huge difference.

But most of all, I get to do the work I do because of the "one in a million" lady I married, Denise. It is Denise and our two daughters— Lauren and Bethany—who always, always love and support me in staying focused and diligent in using the talents God has given me.

Chapter One

Time

Doing too much can mean doing too little.

John wondered, as he drove into Blue Creek High School's parking lot, if this was a good idea. Last year, he had agreed to mentor his successor—as he retired from being the principal at his school. He had grown so much from that experience, but now Dr. Evans, the superintendent, wanted him to mentor all of the principals in the district in a small group format. This cadre would meet once a month for a couple of hours. But in addition, Dr. Evans had given John an additional assignment—a "reclamation project," as he called it. And the project was Todd. Todd was still early in his career, but he showed signs of not being focused enough to lead a school effectively. John's task was to help him discover servant leadership.

"Well, I can't believe it, the master himself is here." Todd tried to appear genuine as he welcomed John into his office. Summer break was nearly over, and the small town high school was bustling with activity. Todd called to the next room and asked one of his assistant principals to handle a parent conference that was scheduled for that afternoon.

"Oh, don't change your schedule around for me, Todd," John urged, and he felt out of place. He wondered if he had written the wrong day or time in his calendar.

"Not a problem, John. I don't need to talk to this lady anyway. She's on my case all the time about this and that. I dodge her every chance I get."

"Well, I'm sure you'll get back to her later, if you're sure it's OK for your assistant to handle it." Todd just stared at John with a look that said: "I don't care to meet with this person—ever again. Now, drop it."

Todd quickly fast forwarded the conversation. "Now John, I understand why the super wants a group of us younger guys to meet with you this year. Great idea. We'll all enjoy it, and it'll get us away from our schools so we can breathe a little. But, I'm curious, why do I really need to do this one-on-one thing with you?"

"Well, Todd, the way I understand it, Dr. Evans sees vast potential in this whole concept of mentoring and coaching. If I were you, I'd look at this as a compliment that he sees potential in you. Let's just take it one visit at a time, and I'm sure it will be a good experience for both of us."

"Well, I'll be honest, John. I don't have time for this. Nothing against you personally, but running a high school is nothing like running an elementary. I'll be surprised if we need to meet more than two or three times. And today, I really need to wrap it up quick, 'cause I promised my buddies I'd meet them for golf in a few minutes. Is there maybe a jumping off point you had thought about discussing first—you know, to get us started?"

John didn't hesitate. "No, I just wanted to chat here in our first visit. But, I know where we need to start. I'll be back next week and I'll need you to only do one thing—show me your calendar, and we'll talk about your philosophy on time management at work."

"Whatever you say big guy. Gotta go. See you next week, same day and time. What—maybe thirty minutes?"

"No, Todd. These will always need to be a minimum of an hour. Have a good golf game today. Sorry I came at what seems to be an inconvenient time."

As John drove home, he thought back to how many times he had rearranged his schedule on the spur of the moment if someone came by to see him or if something else came up that needed his attention. He never remembered rushing anyone out of his office. He never remembered rushing around from project to project, task to task, person to person, and not doing any of it well. He had learned early in his career that school business was a people business.

The joy of the work was not in getting away from the people, but instead being with the people and helping them however he could. He sensed that Todd was already burning out. He sensed that he had been caught up in the overwhelming task of running a high school, but without the tools to do it well and without personal fulfillment. So, John thought about what his task would be over the next several months: to not only perhaps help salvage Todd's career, but also to help him understand and appreciate the role he played as the leader of a school.

* * *

In The Seven Habits of Highly Effective People, *Stephen R. Covey (1989) outlines key principles of personal leadership, which lead to a life of effectiveness and balance in all areas.*

SUMMARY

John realizes that Todd has no interest in a mentoring partnership, even though he has trouble staying focused on how he spends his time wisely at school. In fact, John wonders if Todd even cares about the school and the role he plays as principal. John realizes this is going to be a tough assignment, one he does not look forward to.

Chapter Two

Calendar Management

To simply master self sets everyone else in your life free.

As John drove into the high school's main entrance, he noticed a police car parked just outside the principal's office. He hesitated to go on in, but he wanted to at least let Todd know he had kept his appointment and would reschedule for a better time.

"John, glad you're here!" Todd was pale, nervous, and seemed to be in need of someone to enter the conversation with the officer. After polite introductions, Todd simply blurted out: "Someone's been in here and gotten into my computer and other private files. We're pretty sure it was a student, but no way to know for sure."

"Well, I'm sure this is not the first time this has happened in the school district, Todd. Have you called the superintendent?"

"Not yet."

"Why?"

"'Cause I had left several student files lying on my desk last evening. I meant to file them away where we secure them, but someone I do business with called and needed me to run by their house on my way home, and I just forgot to put them back up."

"But your office was locked, right?"

"I think so, but I can't say for sure. Sometimes I leave it unlocked when in a hurry. The custodians usually lock it for me later in the evening."

Chapter Two

The officer walked to the door. "Call us, Todd, if you think of anything else that would be important for us to know. We'll scan the neighborhood. Often, kids do these things as a prank, and then we find the stuff they stole laying around somewhere. We'll keep you posted."

As the policeman left, Todd just sat back in his chair and ran his hands through his hair with exasperation. "John, how could I have been so stupid? One of those files had info on a kid that would so ruin his reputation in this school if other students found out about the struggle he has had over the years with a sensitive condition. Plus, his psychological tests were in there. Good grief! Why do unusual things like this always happen to me?"

John knew it was not the time to be analyzing further or to be rehashing Todd rushing out of his office the evening before. He just said: "OK. What's done is done. It's possible this was a thief not associated with the school. Call Dr. Evans' office, and your school counselors. Make sure everyone who should be alerted is informed of the situation. I'm going down to take a look at your new gym floor. I hear it's fabulous! Be back in a few minutes."

When John returned, Todd was more composed. But, he kept looking at his watch and shifting in his chair. "John, I hate to tell you this, but I have a hair appointment in thirty minutes."

"Not a good idea today, is it? Why don't you call and reschedule, and then let's take a look at your calendar for this week."

"OK." Todd seemed relieved that John had been assertive and made the decision for him. "Well, I've got one week until opening day, so everything is starting to fill in every spare minute of my time."

John scooted his chair so he could sit beside Todd and asked him to just briefly share his philosophy on how he worked his calendar.

"What do you mean, 'work my calendar'? It just fills up. John, remember—this is a high school. It's always crazy around here, even for much of the summer."

"Tell me about your office staff and other help you have access to."

"Well, let's see, we have our office manager, a secretary, an attendance clerk, our two counselors, two student workers each period of the day, and my two assistant principals."

"So, do you all meet from time to time to go over calendars, and what's coming up?"

"Seldom. They all know their jobs well, John, so I sure don't want to start meeting all the time and adding a bunch of stuff to their plates."

"Well, Todd, I'm just wondering here, as I look at this week on your calendar. It seems a couple of days have huge gaps of time, but then others have something every fifteen minutes all day long. And school's not even started yet. When was the last time you met with your office staff to decide who's going to take care of what and to get their suggestions on planning for the coming year?"

"End of school back in May. Don't worry, John, we'll all get back in here and after school starts, it all seems to work out."

"What about other staff? Do you have a teacher's meeting this week?"

"Yes, but one of my assistant principals takes care of that for me. I assign one of them the staff meetings most of the time, and I assign the other the summer professional development with staff. I figure teachers don't want their boss hanging around in training sessions anyway. Just causes anxiety for the ones who don't like me."

"Well, just a little tip here. If you do have staff who don't like you, all the more reason to be spending more time with them — not less. You need any broken relationships to be healed, for the good of the entire school. And sometimes, what's missing in a principal/teacher relationship is the lack of time spent together working on a common cause."

"Don't agree with you, John. I've coached in this district, I've taught, I've lived in this town all my life. I sure don't need to be pretending I like someone who I indeed don't like or who I know criticizes me behind my back all the time. Now there's a suggestion for you on this time management stuff! I don't waste my time on problem people. I've got more important things to do."

"And Todd, as time goes on, because all of us human folk have issues and blind spots in our personalities, chances are your list of people you don't want to associate with will get longer and longer. It becomes a 'lose, lose' . . . let's talk about your calendar some more. Just briefly explain to me your strategy on how you approach day to day, week to week, month to month here at school."

"Well, what works for me, John, is to keep it simple. So, I come to work every day, I do what I need to do, and I go home. I can retire in about fifteen years, and my philosophy is: 'get 'r done.' And, I'm pretty pleased with how we do things around here. Our football team looks to be one of the best around again this year, we survived graduation again this past spring, we've got kids who are good students. And, those who are losers — well, I find ways to get them out of here. Lots of times they just drop out—quit school. Not fair to have a bunch of jokers in here ruining things for everybody else."

"Well, we've talked enough for today, Todd. I want you to do three things for me this week before the first day of school—just three things. First, meet with your office staff today or tomorrow and talk about anything they need to touch base on before the first day of school, and take a lot of notes on their suggestions for this year. Next, you lead that first teacher's meeting and ask your staff the same thing: What are suggestions for this coming year? In fact, also ask them to write down any other ideas they have and to drop them in your school mailbox. And third, when I come back in two weeks, I want you to have circled on your daily calendar the top three priorities you need to do each day of that week as the principal of this school. Don't schedule any afternoons to leave early to go play golf. Don't schedule any hair appointments during the school day. Keep your daytime hours focused on school. Will you do these three things for me?"

Todd's face turned red, and he started to say something but changed his mind. "John, I will because the superintendent told me to do whatever you asked. Plus, maybe we can get this mentoring thing over with sooner if I can get things checked off your 'to do' list. I gotta go. One of the custodians called in sick, and I just remembered I forgot to call in a sub and we have a truck load of supplies outside. Later."

* * *

In StrengthsFinder 2.0, *Tom Rath (2007) provides guidance for any leader who struggles with allowing weaknesses to get in the way of areas of strongest talent.*

SUMMARY

As John studies Todd's daily calendar, he realizes that his pupil does not have a clue about task management. John gives Todd an assignment that holds him accountable to begin to focus on scheduling his days at school with purpose, including addressing uncomfortable items that he has been avoiding.

Chapter Three

Priorities

If it's important enough to us, it gets done.

As John finished a project his wife had asked him to do around the house, he almost called and cancelled his appointment with Todd. He had dreaded going back to Todd's office. The whole culture of the school was flavored with the attitude that Todd had described so well: "Let's just get 'r done." The secretary, Mrs. Kettering, had not been friendly on John's first two visits; the front lobby had been messy and in disarray; staff and students would pass him in the hallway and not speak. So, John was shocked when the secretary actually greeted him with a smile and warm welcome.

"Todd, I want to compliment Mrs. Kettering. She went out of her way just now to greet me with top notch customer service."

"Well, I must confess. I thought your list you gave me to do on your last visit was just that: a list that I really didn't have time for. But John, the office staff here loved our last team meeting. I was busy and had not even had time to make notes for an agenda, so I remembered you said to ask them for suggestions for the coming year. We had the most awesome conversation as a group we've ever had. In fact, I mostly listened. Once the ideas started flowing, they just kept coming. And the main thing we decided was we all had to do a better job here in the office of having things looking nice and pleasant and also being nice to people."

John about fainted and dared to ask how the teacher's meeting went. "John, the teachers loved the opportunity to make suggestions to me as the ideas came to them. So, I've had a lot of notes being dropped in my mailbox this week. But, I don't have time to look at them right now—maybe sometime this fall. And, I must confess—I haven't had time to circle the top three priorities for each day of this week, but I did this morning do today and tomorrow's so you could take a look."

"Ok, let's see what you've done." John was so happy about the first two tasks being completed that he excused Todd's not completing the third. At least, he had started it.

"Todd, I see three items circled for today. Your meeting with me, lunch with the coaches, and a meeting at central office to discuss bid prices for this year. I'm curious, could one of your assistants cover that bid meeting for you?"

"Well, yeah, I guess. I just have always gone to that one, but I don't really have to be there as long as one of us from here shows up."

"I was just thinking, having that extra time in that meeting slot would allow you to start looking over the suggestions your staff have been giving you. Since you have them communicating with you like this, what an opportunity to build some momentum."

"But John, honestly, I don't know where to start. They've made so many suggestions already."

"But this does not have to be all on your shoulders. In fact, it shouldn't be. When's your next school advisory council meeting?"

"Next Tuesday after school."

"Why don't you look over the suggestions and keep looking over them as they come in, and have them in a nice list for your council to look at next week. Then, perhaps the council will even want to appoint a separate team from your faculty, students, and parents to work on how best to rank these priorities, and when and how to start plugging them in. They all don't have to be done now. Some may be even better to work on second semester or in getting ready for next school year."

"Good idea, but typing the list up, with all the other interruptions in my typical day, will take two or three hours. You ought to see it!"

"And you have an office manager, secretary, and student workers in here every day, correct?"

"Yes I do. I guess I could find someone to help on this."

"Also Todd, I love the idea of meeting with your coaches for lunch. Do you also meet with teacher teams, your cafeteria staff, your custodians, your PTA officers, your student council, or other members of your school community?"

"No, just the coaches for lunch every few days. With the others, they know I will meet with them if they ask, but I have not worked in their shoes, so I just don't feel comfortable forcing them to have a 'pow wow' with me."

"Well, you know what? I can almost guarantee that your coaches appreciate the time you take just to sit down and have a meal with them more than you would ever know. Your assignment over the next two weeks: schedule lunches with these other teams too. In fact, let's put it on your calendar right now as a 'must do' this week—to get these team lunches scheduled as soon as possible."

"But John, I don't have time to contact all these people and work this out! I hate scheduling and am not good at it. This would take me weeks and weeks."

"Not if you commit to it on your calendar, and after you get the ball rolling, give it to someone here in the office who can take care of the details."

"Ok, I'll do it. And, before you leave, want to ask you about something that came up this week. The superintendent, Dr. Evans, called over here one day and informed me that the school board was rotating their monthly meetings this year from school to school. He wanted to schedule our school for next month, and besides that, wanted me to do some type of presentation that showcases our school."

"Wow, what an opportunity to feature your school at a board meeting. What are you going to do your presentation on?"

"Nothing. I put him off and said we absolutely could not host a meeting this fall, and would try to manage it in the spring. But, if he would let me out of it, I'd prefer to not have our school in the rotation."

"Todd, why did you turn him down? Why not host the meeting next month as you were asked to and recruit some staff to help you put a nice presentation together?"

"Because I hate board meetings, I hate night meetings here at the school, and I hate speaking in public—especially to the board. Besides, what's the board done for me lately anyway? Seems to me all they do is put pressure on us to keep trying to get better and better as a school, and it's unreasonable."

"They put a new floor on your gym this summer didn't they? I'll see you in a couple of weeks." John turned back as he reached for the door. "Todd, leaders are in the business of building bridges, not burning them."

* * *

In The One Minute Manager, *Ken Blanchard and Spencer Johnson (1982) offer simple, effective strategies for supervisors in setting and monitoring goals for self and staff.*

SUMMARY

Todd begins to pay attention to John's advice and sees some surprising success as he asks for suggestions from his staff all around the building. John notices a difference in the culture as soon as he is greeted by a friendlier secretary and is also pleased to see that Todd has indeed begun prioritizing his daily planner.

Chapter Four

Integrity Heals the Culture

When we live from the inside out, when we do the right thing just because it is the right thing to do, we have overcome life's temptation to take shortcuts. Shortcuts often lead to a dark forest of no return—a maze of contradictions that cause us to finally realize we are a shell of the man (or woman) we used to be.

September was here, and John was on his way to a meeting with the superintendent. He was to give an update on the leadership cadre he was facilitating with the district's principals and also to discuss the progress he was having with Todd. What he would find out in the next hour made him sick to his stomach. He wondered if he even wanted to do this mentoring stuff anymore. On his drive to Todd's school, he simply prayed to not judge, but to listen and have a lot of grace.

"Come in, John. Well, how's my ol' buddy? Can't wait to tell you how much better I feel about how I'm prioritizing my daily calendar. Everyone around the building is telling me they have noticed a difference."

"Todd, I need to discuss something else with you first. I just came from the superintendent's office, and audits of your school's books show that you all may have taken unethical liberties with one of your grants last year. The super thinks he can work this out with the grant agency to not press charges, but oh my, is he hot. Fill me in."

"What? Don't know what he's talking about. We only had one new grant funding anything around here last year, and that was the state math 'booster,' as they called it. I wasn't even involved with that project. I let the math department take care of all the details."

"Who signed off on the expenses?"

"Well, I guess I did. But my secretary brings bills in here every few days. Sometimes I sign twenty or thirty at a time. I don't look at the details, I just sign."

"Well, somebody in this school used a considerable amount of that funding to pay for field trips that weren't truly part of the grant, to pay some extra salary to tutors who weren't written into the grant, and an ice cream machine for the cafeteria was even purchased with the grant."

"Oh John, come on. All schools do things like this all the time. The grant folks know how bad we need the money. I remember the ice cream machine. We purchased it so we could give the kids a party after they did so well on the spring exams, which included improvement on our math scores. So, it was related."

"Todd, surely you know better. All schools do not misuse funds from grants! Do you realize how fortunate you all are that Dr. Evans has worked this out without severe penalties levied on your school and this district? However, he did say the district would have to pay several thousand dollars back to make up for the illicit spending. What if he decides that your school will pay this out of your funds? Where will you get the money?"

"Well, I guess we could dip into the PTA surplus fund that the district office doesn't know about. Or we could borrow from our petty cash fund we have built up from the sale of pop and candy. It's grown to a few thousand dollars over the years. We try to keep that quiet too by keeping a lot of it in a separate private account at the bank. Never know when you'll need it for a rainy day."

John decided to probe further, as he realized the math grant was only the tip of the iceberg. "Sounds like some shrewd planning. Any other tips on how to beat the system in use of financial resources?"

"Well, I know I wouldn't be able to have the coaching staff I have if not for hiring people to teach social studies or PE, but then actually giving them a half day of planning and to work with their kids in what we call 'team sport' class. The state athletic association says we can't do this, but my coaches tell me it's done all the time across the state."

"Wow, no wonder your teams are winning championships every year. Any other 'tricks of the trade'?"

"Sure, lots more. Maybe you'd let me share these in our next principal's cadre session. One thing we do that is brilliant that I learned from the last guy who was principal here is to not use sick days. The way he saw it, if he was here for even thirty minutes on a day he was sick, and then went home, it should count since he worked a lot of long days with this job. So, when he retired, the district owed him several thousand dollars in unused sick days he'd saved over the years."

"Did he not realize the district had built into his contract extra salary for his extended time at work?"

"I don't know. He just said that everybody does it, and it sure builds up a lot of sick days over a period of years."

"Any other shortcuts?"

"Well, sometimes we can build in bonuses for staff if they are willing to stay after school to cover detention."

"Bonuses?"

"Sure. We have some tutoring funds provided by the state every year. We simply set aside some of those dollars for our after-school detention hall. Makes great sense, and the staff love the extra cash."

"Do they know they are being paid from funds that are set aside for tutoring, not for an after-school discipline program?"

"No, I don't make it complicated, John. The money's there, and I use it the way I see fit."

"Anything else? What about being reimbursed for school trips, meals, things like that?"

"Oh sure. When I go on trips down state, I can make a pretty good profit if I want to."

"How's that?"

"Well, let's say the conference includes meals that are provided. I get to eat those meals, then still turn in my food allotment expense for the day."

"Todd, in case you've not checked, and I truly hope you have just not known any better, everything you've told me here is against ethical fiscal policy for a school or school district."

"John, chill out. There's nothing wrong with it. It's called making up for being in a career that grossly underpays its employees."

"No, Todd. It's called cheating."

* * *

In The Cheating Culture, *David Callahan (2004) addresses the dilemma of breaking the rules and taking ethical shortcuts that plagues U.S. culture. He places the blame largely on the vicious economics of our generation.*

SUMMARY

As John gets to know Todd better, he is sickened by the younger principal's disregard for the proper use of school funds. Todd has learned to beat the system and seems surprised when John reminds him that several financial practices he has endorsed at his school are unethical.

Chapter Five

"Barnyard" Politics

Accepting the theory of "it's not what you know, it's who you know" has led many a man down a road of mediocrity and compromise, and eventually not having a clue what to do when it's his turn to stand tall in the midst of adversity.

Todd lost a lot of sleep over what John had said about cheating and called him at home a couple of days later. "John, do you play golf?"

"No, but I love to fish."

"Super. I'm taking you out on the lake this Saturday. Pick you up about 7 A.M. if you want to go."

"I'll be ready."

Todd was anxious to clear things up, and didn't waste any time before trying to make an apology as soon as they had the boat in the water and were settled in a good spot for bass. "John, you're a good man. And I must be honest with you, even though I thought you coming by school to chat this year would be such a waste of time, you've helped me. I've learned a couple of things already about how to better manage my time at work. About what I said the other day—I just figured you saw those examples as another way of being a good manager. I had no idea you felt so strongly about the gray areas."

"Son, life is all about the gray areas. My daddy told me a long time ago that when you can fudge on the little things, after awhile, they all seem like little things. He told me that if I ever wanted to amount to anything in this world, I would have to decide if my principles would drive me or if my human nature to do what was convenient and less painful would drive me. He was right."

"But John, don't you think if a man is not hurting anybody, that sometimes you can sort of do both? It's like not turning in everything on my income taxes. Who does that hurt?"

"It hurts our society. It hurts your parents who raised you better than that. It hurts your wife and two precious little boys. It hurts your school, and everyone who believes in you and looks up to you Todd."

"Just over a few dollars that the government probably owes me anyway?"

"What did you bring for lunch, Todd?"

"Oh, just a couple of sandwiches and a candy bar."

"What if I ate your candy bar without asking you first? After all, it only costs fifty cents—almost nothing. And what if I never owed up to it? We went home later, you dropped me off, and I never bothered to tell you I'd 'taken' your candy bar."

"I wouldn't mind giving you the bar, John, but I would mind that you respected me so little that you stole it, instead of going by the social rules we live by and asking for it politely."

"And that's the whole point, Todd. If, as a culture, we all start fudging on this and that, because we assume no one will notice or get hurt—after a while, there are no boundaries. And eventually, we become a society of distrust and chaos."

"OK, John, then tell me what to do about this situation I find myself in. The other day, you reminded me that our school board had put a new floor on our gym this summer. What if I told you that I know the board member personally who made that recommendation in a board meeting last spring, and one reason we got that new floor is because his daughter is a senior this year, and he wants her being homecoming queen real bad? What if I told you he and I sort of have a deal going on? No one's getting hurt. The school gets a new gym floor, and his daughter gets five minutes of fame during halftime of our homecoming game later this fall."

"What if there is another little girl more deserving?"

"Well, we'll get her named something else special later on this year. What if I told you I get to count the votes, and I can make it right as the year goes on for any of the girls who finish high on the list?"

"Todd, listen to what you're saying. You're tainting the process so what the people at that game think is reality is only an illusion. And, you are making a mockery of every student who casts a vote."

"Well, John, don't worry. I can't stand the whole homecoming queen thing anyway, so I'm not going to do it. But, I can tell you, the board member hinted to me he expected favors in return this year."

"You scratch my back, I'll scratch yours."

"Exactly. John, don't take this the wrong way, 'cause you're a super guy. I admire you greatly. But you do appear somewhat naive. This type of stuff goes on all the time. My granddaddy was a state representative, and he said in politics you live and die by tradeoffs and compromise. And I've seen it so much in my work as a coach and now a principal."

"But, Todd, there's a difference in good politics and bad politics. Good politics does involve compromise and everybody working for 'win, win.' But bad politics does it underhandedly, by cheating and doing things in ways that are unethical."

"So, to be a little corny here, it's not if you win or lose, but how you play the game?"

"Yes, Todd. You used to be a coach. Isn't that what you taught your players? You worked them hard, taught them well, and after a game, if they had done their best, you sent them home with a pat on the back and that was the end of it."

"Most of the time, John, but I'll be honest. In today's world of obsessed parents, and the high stakes of winning, it becomes real hard to not take advantage in a game any way you can."

"Well, you're not coaching anymore. And you're not a board member or a state representative. In these next few years, as a school principal, you have such an opportunity, Todd, to make a huge difference in your school and community by simply doing everything by the book, totally on the level—the right way."

"Oh John, again, you're so naïve. I'm not an education guru. I'm not a curriculum specialist or a person who can walk down the halls and everybody wants to talk to me and shake my hand. I can barely stand up in front of the student body on opening day and welcome them back to school. I'm a man who gets paid to police and manage my school. I am not what all the books say is a strong school leader."

"You have so much potential, Todd! We've just got to drill down to your instincts of 'goodness' that you've allowed to be buried inside for too long and start putting your talents to work."

"And where do I start, John?" Todd turned away to the other side of the boat and John thought he heard his voice crack.

"You've already started. Let's catch some fish."

* * *

In Ethics—The Heart of Leadership, *Joanne Ciulla (1998) delves deep into the core values of leading with principles and character, not just skills and the ability, at whatever cost, to get the job done.*

SUMMARY

While on a fishing outing to get away and talk heart to heart, Todd shares that a board member is expecting him to rig the voting so his daughter is named homecoming queen. This opens the door for John to teach in depth about the basics of right and wrong, and the role a leader plays in protecting others from careless leadership.

Chapter Six

Instructional Support

Every child has many gifts to share with this world. If we can't help them discover those gifts after working with them for fourteen years, maybe the problem is not with the child, but with the system.

Todd wished he had postponed John's next visit. Blue Creek High was in the middle of football season, and he was focused on the team. He had fulfilled John's request to meet with the various small groups of staff around the building and felt like he had a better handle on his calendar and priorities than ever before. But in football season, these mentoring sessions were becoming a distraction to his busy schedule.

"Come in, John, and grab a seat. I may be running in and out this morning. Lots of stuff going on. I thought I'd leave my calendar out for you to look at, so you can check off the areas where I have followed up on your tasks."

"Sounds like a good idea. You just go do what you have to do and maybe we can sit down and talk for a few minutes later after I've made some notes."

John was thrilled to see that Todd was highlighting his top priorities for each day and that he had indeed met with several teams of his staff over lunch. And his eyebrows rose with pleasant surprise when he saw that Todd had written in an October school council item called "internal budget monitoring team," with representatives from all around the building to be selected to assist. John had wondered if their discussions on ethics and leaving the door open for manipulation of funds would lead to any changes in policy. Apparently, Todd listened.

But as John thumbed through Todd's planner, he saw practically nothing involving instruction. He could not find evidence of Todd's meeting with content teams, department chairs, attending instructional meetings on district level, or regional or state conferences. In fact, he thought maybe Todd kept a separate calendar for this area of his job.

Todd rushed in. "John, I've got about twenty minutes tops, then we're having a pep rally. So, what you got?"

"Well, I love what I see on organization. You've followed through on specific strategies we had talked about. Just stay with it. But I don't see much of anything on instructional leadership. Do you keep a separate calendar or planner for that?"

"No, I just have not had time yet this year to do much of that, John. It's football season. Besides, I have a competent staff—they know what they're doing."

"Would you say that's true for your football coaches, too?"

"Oh yeah—one of the best coaching staffs around."

"So, you *do* provide more support to these guys than you do other teacher teams?"

"Well now, John, I wouldn't look at it that way. The staff all know I'm a sports nut. Plus, like I told you previously, my assistants take care of all that stuff I don't want to deal with."

"All that 'stuff'?"

"Yeah, you know—reading, math, academic team, Beta club."

"Todd, it's fine to delegate a lot to your assistants and your other help. That's a wise use of time and resources *if* you're making sure you're right there with as much support for your other programs as you are for the sports program."

"I assure you, John, they understand. Like I said, we all do a pretty good job around here."

"Just because you're sure they understand doesn't mean your absence in curriculum meetings and in all these other parts of this complex system called a high school isn't noticed *and* missed. You mentioned reading and math a moment ago. Well, guess what? High school math scores across the board are shockingly low, not only in this region but also across the state and country. Many high school kids still can't read well, and that's why a bunch of them drop out as soon as they hit ninth or tenth grade. And this is not including the dismal student data on other core courses."

"But what am I supposed to do about that, John? I'm only one person, and I'm not a math or reading guru."

"No, but you're the leader of this school. Your support matters. Your staff, your students, their parents, and the community need to see you behind every student service this school has to offer."

"You show me where to start then, John! I'm swamped right now and that won't change until Christmas break. You've never run a high school. How would you know what the pressure cooker's really like in this chair?" Todd was mad, and his face was red. John had pushed pretty hard, but he knew he needed to, especially if he was going to help Todd take the reins of this school.

"Todd, I need you to take on just one new task in the next two weeks. Use your office help here to assist, and develop a student survey that will give your kids in this high school the freedom to express how they feel about the total menu of services here. Tally up the results, and when I return in October, we'll talk about the survey."

"Oh, John, get real. Kids don't take this stuff seriously. Half of them will throw such a survey in the trash can! And the other half? Who knows what they'll write down!"

"So you're scared to do the survey?"

"No, but I think it'll be a waste of time."

"Do you all do exit interviews here with your seniors as they graduate?"

"No. The seniors just want to get out of here and get on with life. We can barely get them to come to school those last few weeks."

"So, really, you haven't a clue what your kids in this building really think about their school, do you?"

"John, we talk to them every day. I spend time with them at lunch, on ball trips. I even know a lot of them by their first name."

"You mean you know a lot of the athletes by their first name, and probably the troublemakers who are in the office all the time being written up for misbehaving."

"No, I mean I know what these kids will do, and what they won't do. I know what they want in a high school."

"So then, doing the survey shouldn't be a problem, should it?"

"OK, OK. If you'll then give it a rest, John, I'll do the survey! Good grief, man, you're taking this mentoring thing way too seriously!"

* * *

In The Visionary's Handbook—Nine Paradoxes That Will Shape the Future of Your Business, *Jim Taylor and Watts Wacker (2000) reveal that leaders who have the greatest impact on the future embrace unconventional strategies that go against the accepted norm.*

SUMMARY

As Todd and John move through the fall semester, John notices that Todd does little work in the area of instructional support. He seems to be intimidated by his lack of technical know how and delegates this part of his job whenever he can. John pushes him to survey the student body, asking for ideas about how to improve the school.

Chapter Seven

Students Know What Is Missing

They are mere "pups," so eager to taste the sweetness of new learning. They have visions, and hopes, and dreams. And they are also awkward, unsure—so easily bruised. Sometimes as one observes up and down the hallways, the school does not look like a learning center at all, but instead resembles a huge mall, with the nameless faces hinting that they have accepted the reality that these are simply the rites of passage—however irrelevant and uninspiring.

The autumn brought with it a magical trip to the mountains with his wife and kids, and John came back renewed—and eager to see Todd's student surveys. As John began explaining where he had been the last few days, a distant, almost sad look came over Todd's face.

"I'd love to have the time to do trips like that with my boys. John, when you were a principal, did you ever feel like you were neglecting your family?"

"Yes, at first. Then I realized that to be a leader at school, I needed to be a leader at home first. After making that commitment to my family, everything changed at work. I was able to finally let go of the preoccupation with self and get my life's priorities straight. After all, what would it mean to be the hero to every child in my school, but later find out my kids didn't even know me?"

"I bet you're a great husband and father, John." Todd looked down and shifted his eyes toward the window. John sensed that he was realizing personal gaps in the dual roles he played in running a school and in being the family man he needed to be at home.

"Well, I'm curious my boy. What did the kids have to say about Blue Creek High School?"

"John, I just never dreamed . . . " Todd reached for the summary of the student surveys and read down the list item by item. "The kids say that a lot of our classes are boring. They say that we aren't teaching math well, thus we lose them when the more advanced concepts come along. They get angry when their classmates who are poor readers are asked to read aloud or are ignored in the back of the room as if they aren't even there. They want adults in this school to care enough to not give up on these students and let them drop out."

Todd nodded his head, agreeing but almost as if embarrassed, then went on. "They want more counselors who will have time to help them with a variety of issues ranging from peer pressure to being prepared for going after college scholarships. They admit that we have a serious subculture here at Blue Creek of harassment and bullying. The only students not being harassed in some way are the jocks."

"Oh, I'm just getting started, John. This survey blew me away. They want more clubs. They wish we'd offer intramurals and not just varsity sports. They wish we'd invest more resources and time into the arts. They don't like too much study hall. They don't know what to do when a classmate has an addiction problem. They beg for more technology. They want to take some classes online from home, in the evenings, and on weekends, so they would have the option to take more electives during their four years here. They would like to have smaller classes so they could get to know their teachers better."

"And I guess I'd just never thought this one through, but some say we have a double standard for athletes and cheerleaders. Wow, that one really bothers me. They want more 'real life' experiences, more field trips to learn about careers, exposure to leaders from the community. They want more guidance on 'life' skills—like managing a personal budget, how to make better choices, how to manage their time better, how to cultivate hobbies, and how to take notes and study in prep for college. They are so tired of the classes in which they sit and the information is poured into them. They want to be 'doing' science, actively learning history, being taught how to write better."

"The last one here made me just slink down in my chair and want to go home. This kid wrote: 'In elementary school, up to about third grade, learning was fun. Now, I just go along in every class so I can get done and go home as soon as the afternoon bell rings. I learn at home on my computer. At school, I just breathe and hang on.'"

John calmly smiled, stood up, and went over and patted Todd on the back. "And now Todd, you have all you need to truly transform this school."

"How, John? Good gravy, this is depressing, and there's no way we can do even one-fourth of these things!"

"Well, one-fourth this year, and one-fourth next year, and before you know it, you've got a great school on your hands."

"A school run by kids, is that it, John?"

"No, a school designed truly for the kids. A school that piques their interests, provides experiential, relevant learning for them much like when they go to camp in the summer and don't want to come home. A school that breaks down all the traditional barriers that kill a lot of these students' thirst for knowledge and instead gets totally focused on meeting their needs and getting them ready for life."

"Oh, it sounds exciting, all right! In reality, the staff would laugh at making such changes."

"How many staff, Todd, do you estimate would not take this feedback from the student body seriously and then jump in and make adjustments in better meeting their needs?"

"Oh, out of forty teachers around the building, there are ten who would buck this all the way."

"Would you let twenty-five percent block the success of the football team?"

"No."

"Then, why don't you consider putting together another new team, as you did with your budget monitoring team? Simply call it the 'dream' team. Include students and parents on it. Start meeting with the purpose of looking at what the students have said are gaps in this school. Todd, you'll be amazed at what will begin to happen."

"Can this be my last new task for a while?"

"Well, let's just go one week at a time. I will say this: The most important thing you have done this entire semester, by far, is this student survey. I am proud of you, and you are onto something here that some schools never figure out."

Todd didn't leap for joy, but he didn't complain or frown either. He just had a look as if a light had come on in his head—the first time John had seen it. And John smiled inside.

"I better go . . . oh, Todd, one more thing. Why don't you go home and talk to your family about a fall trip. I'll speak to Dr. Evans about me filling in here at school for you on a Thursday and Friday, so you can take your gang on a long weekend."

For the first time, Todd reached out and shook John's hand. "I'll do it."

* * *

In Schools That Learn, *Peter Senge (2000) provides a comprehensive outline of what a school can look like if totally focused on each student learning and learning well. Somehow, our schooling system on a macro level often gets lost in so much around the fringe that it is not meeting the learning needs of the children who are entrusted to our care.*

SUMMARY

When the results of the student survey are tallied, Todd is shocked at the many gaps in the total menu of school services the students identify. He does not know where to begin to address the issues, but John sees something crucial beginning to take place: Todd is starting to get it.

Chapter Eight

Holding Teachers Accountable

> *A teacher can be a role model and mentor that a student never forgets, with the positive impact lasting a lifetime. And a "teacher" can forget why he or she is even working with students, thus wreaking havoc on the culture of creativity, trusting relationships, and learning.*

The dynamics of running a healthy school, as with any organization, depend heavily on all stakeholders being committed to the vision and being willing to get out of the way so new ideas can flourish. John knew that if Todd followed up on the student survey, initially the school would be filled with tension because the human nature of resisting change would rear its ugly head. As he thought about his next visit, he knew it would be critical for Todd to see beyond the "political correctness" of keeping the status quo happy.

"John, I can't thank you enough for covering for me here so I could get away with my family. Best thing I've done in a long, long time."

"Well, I hope the ship was still in one piece when you returned, Todd. I relied on all your staff and I mainly just made myself available for unusual stuff and emergencies. Fortunately, everything seemed to go fine."

"John, I received a lot of compliments from folks all over the building, staff and students alike, about how friendly you were and how they enjoyed getting to know you. You have a gift for making people feel comfortable and appreciated."

"I just try to see things from the other person's perspective, Todd. That one rule has helped me so much over the years in dealing with all the complicated things that come up in school work."

"Well then, is that how you would advise I handle the student survey? I did as you suggested and met yesterday after school with a newly formed 'dream' team. Their purpose is to simply consider ways that we can better meet student needs here at Blue Creek."

"Sounds like you're right on target."

"But remember that ten percent we talked about?"

"You mean the resisters?"

"Yep. They're at it already today. Seems someone has called for a 'teachers-only' meeting after school, and someone else has started a petition to voice staff displeasure of my leadership to the school board."

"Because of one student survey?"

"Because we are taking the student survey seriously."

"Todd, tell me something. Have you been doing 'walkthroughs'?"

"What's a 'walkthrough'?"

"Just a simple process for a principal to use in becoming more familiar with classroom instruction. Some principals even chart what they observe as they document several visits a year to each classroom. Really helps later on, too, when going over evaluations and developing growth plans."

"John, I wouldn't know where to start. I would feel so intimidated. Plus, I have two or three who basically don't measure up to the rest, so I'd just be opening up a whole new can of worms."

"What do you mean?"

"You know—dead weight. I have one teacher who doesn't even dress professionally anymore. He comes in late, leaves early, and misses meetings. Students and parents tell me all the time that he mainly sits at his desk and has the kids do work sheets or gives them study hall."

"How long has he been here, Todd?"

"Oh, about twenty years. He's one of the ones who is all worked up over the student survey, too."

"Any other weak links on your staff you care to tell me about?"

"Well, I have a new teacher who is struggling a lot it seems. This is her first year, and the district did not get her mentor assigned until last week. She has no control in the classroom. The kids just make fun of her."

"Anybody else?"

"Well, I have a teacher who has a bad reputation for flirting with the girls. He has had a couple of close calls with parents threatening to turn him into authorities for sexual harassment."

"Why is he still employed by the district?"

"'Cause his father is a millionaire and an icon in this community. No one will touch the issue with a ten-foot pole."

"I guess you know you're required to investigate this further if you have any suspicions, don't you?"

"John, I don't remember saying I have any suspicions. May all just be rumors. That's my stance on this—I have a family to support. Besides, what about my ol' school 'boss' down the hall who yells at her students all the time? She doesn't want us to do anything different unless it's her idea, and frankly, she makes me nervous just to be around her. I know she talks about me behind my back all the time. But if I was going to investigate student harassment, I'd have to investigate her, too. Everybody knows she loses it in front of the kids sometimes, and she's even been known to physically get aggressive with students—you know, down in their face, perhaps too firm a hand on the shoulder, or even an occasional shove up against a locker."

"Todd, if I created a 'walkthrough' instrument for you to use for the rest of the year, would you try it—just to see if it helps you to be more on top of instruction and to develop some good communication with you and your teachers? Plus, I'm sure the students would love seeing you in and out of the classrooms more, too."

"Do I have a choice?"

"If you are really serious about addressing the gaps in this school, I don't think you have a choice *not* to."

"Well, it would be good to have more to talk about when I have my evaluation conferences each spring. And it would be wonderful if the staff would develop growth plans that were real and meaningful."

"Exactly. And, you'll be amazed what you will find out about the culture of this school just by walking around like this and taking notes."

"Plus, it would force me to get to know staff better, and they would get to know me better. And I'd get to see in detail what the kids are doing in their classes. I always mean to get more involved with their work, but I never seem to have the time."

"Well, here's your chance."

"But, John, won't teachers feel threatened by this? Won't they view this as a way for me to catch them up in poor teaching?"

"Actually, let's not frame it that way at all. Let's call it your 'catching folks doing something good' walks—for staff and students."

"But when will I find the time, John?"

"Todd, you and your assistant principals will all have to shift your priorities as needed if the student survey is to be taken seriously. This is a great chance for you to move some of the less important tasks off of your plate."

"Well, I must confess, I spend a lot of time here in the office waiting for work to come to me. Often, it becomes crisis management—fires to be put out."

"Time to change that, Todd. You're so much more than just a crisis manager."

* * *

In Leading from the Inside Out, *Samuel Rima (2000) dives into the dark reality that many folks in leadership positions are not skilled at first leading themselves. Thus, inwardly spiraling out of control, such a careless leader becomes a liability to the organization, and sooner or later hurts those around him or her.*

SUMMARY

As Todd begins to accept his responsibility to truly provide leadership for his school, he confides in John regarding two teachers who are not ethically qualified to be working with students. John suggests that Todd begin doing "walkthroughs," observing teachers at work in their classrooms and becoming visible as a principal who is paying attention to instructional practices.

Chapter Nine

Abusers of Children

They come and go, hundreds of children and youth, day after day. Their parents and all of society naturally assume that we are taking care of them well, protecting them fiercely, and never letting one hand harm them in any way.

John had trouble sleeping as he thought about the examples Todd had given him of staff abusing kids. He decided he could not let go of what he had been told without some type of intervention. The lazy teacher was fixable. The overwhelmed new teacher was fixable. But the verbally abusive teacher and the possible sexual predator? He wondered if he should consult with the superintendent. But first, he wanted to meet these educators, who apparently had somehow gotten away with mistreatment of students for years.

Initially, Todd was not too keen on John observing any of his staff, but he obliged once he realized this was a great way to get comfortable with the "walkthroughs." He purposely saved the two teachers John had specifically asked to meet until last. And it did not take long for John to witness some unsettling behavior because Mrs. Walker could be heard yelling well down the hallway.

"Todd, does she do this all the time?"

"Pretty much every day, I'm told."

"And no one has been able to put a stop to this?"

"Oh, they've tried. The last principal tried. Several parents have complained to the board. A few students have pleaded for help over the years. But, John, let's be realistic. She has tenure. Who's going to challenge her and win?"

As the two entered the classroom, Mrs. Walker had just written a question on the board and was waiting for students to hold up their hands to respond. When no one volunteered, she called on a shy boy in the back of the room: "Tommy, time to wake up. Sit up in your chair now and let's show our principal and our other guest who have surprised us this morning without warning that we are studying and learning in here all the time. Say something smart now, not something stupid."

Tommy just froze, and every other student in the room seemed to slide down in their chairs as Mrs. Walker looked at the class with a stone glare. Then she looked at Todd and John with a similar glare. Todd just waved, and the two left the room immediately.

On the other end of the hallway, Todd stopped before entering Mr. Crow's room. "John, he's slick. You'd never suspect he flirts with the girls in his classes all the time." Mr. Crow was at his desk, and the class seemed to be having some free study time. Kids were moving about the room, and three or four were around his desk talking to him. Two girls were on either side of his desk in their chairs, as if they had been especially assigned to sit up front.

"Hello, Mr. Crow. We've been taking a tour of our classrooms this morning. John here has been mentoring me this year."

"Hello, gentlemen. Glad you came by. We're just getting ready to take our unit test tomorrow, so the kids are doing some final test prep today. Anything I can do for you?"

John immediately replied: "Yes, I'd like to interview some of your students about how they like this course. How about if I borrowed these two here sitting beside your desk for a few minutes? We'll just take them down to the office, and I'll send them back in a jiffy."

The look on Mr. Crow's face spoke volumes, as John had followed a hunch and called him out. "Well, uh, really, they need to be studying for the exam. How about later, say next week?"

"Well, that will work too. If we are going to wait that long, why don't we just interview all your students next week? I've been helping your principal here compile data on the school, and interviewing an entire class would really be helpful. I'll get back with you on the details."

As John and Todd walked back to the office, John simply asked: "What if the superintendent opens an investigation on both of these teachers? It seems to me, based on what others have told you repeatedly, there's enough doubt that you have no choice, Todd."

"Will I be protected, John? I won't get in trouble, will I?"

"How could you get in trouble?"

"Well, I've heard stories of how these things turn into one big mess, and the truth gets twisted around until the bad guys are made to look like the good guys, and vice versa."

"Todd, do you want abusive teachers in your school?"

"No, of course not."

"Then, let's just see what Dr. Evans wants to do."

The next morning, the superintendent instructed his district office staff to conduct extensive interviews with current students, parents, and staff and also past students, parents, and staff regarding the "classroom practices" of both Mrs. Walker and Mr. Crow. Within a few days, multiple testimonies revealed strong evidence that Mrs. Walker had verbally abused students in her classroom for years. There were also examples cited of her being too physically aggressive with students. Likewise, much came to the surface on Mr. Crow's obsessive attraction to the females in his classes. The evidence was so strong against both teachers that Dr. Evans decided to start the process for dismissal. Mr. Crow resigned immediately. Mrs. Walker announced that she was retiring at mid-year.

As Todd spoke to John from his cell phone as he left for a Friday evening football trip out of town, it was obvious he was still in shock: "I still can't believe it, John. Those two had gotten away with this stuff for years, and no one had ever even questioned them apparently. What made the difference this time?"

"This time, Todd, when the suspicions were relayed to the superintendent, he decided to do all he could do. He's been cleaning up the nonsense in this district for several months now, and this is just one more example. Neither one of us really had any choice in the matter, did we? If we are to be the leaders hired to protect the children of this community, did we really have another option?"

"I never thought of it that way, John. I guess you're right. I had just always seen my role as the protector of the staff. Never really thought much about who was there to protect the students who were victims of careless staff. I'm a little ashamed."

"Don't be, Todd. You, too, have been a victim of a broken system that has become so self-serving in some ways over the years it has not been mature enough to police itself. Plus, you have helped root out the problem here in this school. You can hold your head high. There are other abuses in other schools, and those are the issues we must encourage our colleagues down in the trenches to have the courage to address and not ignore any longer."

"I can't stop thinking about those poor kids being harassed and yet too scared to even know what to do. And how many have cried out for help, but no one listened?"

"And what if one of them had been your child, Todd, or mine? Sweeping the cancer under the rug doesn't get rid of it. It just lets it hide until someone else gets hurt. In our school systems and other organizations across our society, we've got to care enough for the victims to stare the cancer square in the eye and simply say: 'No more'."

* * *

In Leadership and Self-Deception, *the Arbinger Institute (2000) discloses harsh realities about how easy it is for individuals to not see their careless tendencies as others see them. Thus, with such blind spots allowed to continue unchecked, unhealthy relationships and hurt to others often result.*

SUMMARY

In spending time in classrooms, Todd and John observe enough questionable behavior from two teachers that they ask the superintendent for assistance. With the support of the district office, the two are exposed. One resigns, and the other retires. Todd begins to realize that principle-driven leaders do not really have a choice to protect staff that are unfit for the classroom by sweeping student and parental complaints under the rug.

Chapter Ten

Jocks

They are innocent, these children, and look to their teachers as beacons of all that is good. They don't understand when they see us look the other way, as we protect ourselves, while our principles and our souls erode away.

As Thanksgiving approached, John and Todd's conversations had gone to a new level of trust, as both had walked on hot coals during this semester of deep probing into the true culture of Blue Creek High School. Todd had less of a swagger to his walk, but his steps had more purpose than before. He spent less time looking for ways to get out of work and instead was learning to face huge challenges head on. Thus, he did not carry an air of pretense, but instead an air of realness—an air of principle. It was football playoff time, and Todd had hoped the rest of the year could be smooth sailing. But, that all changed when his head football coach asked him for a special favor.

"Come in, John, sit down. Have a donut." Todd seemed nervous.

"You OK, son? Bet you all around here are excited about the playoffs starting this weekend."

"Oh my, yes! You know, John, we have a chance to win it all this year. The coaches tell me if we get by this first game, we might just win a state championship! So, when they put it to me that way, I certainly could see their point about Bucky Jones."

"Bucky Jones? Your halfback? One of the best in the state . . . he's not injured, is he?"

"No, no, thank goodness. But he's had some problems keeping up in a couple of classes. I've got it all worked out though."

"All worked out?"

"Yep. Seems he's failing senior English and biology. But, I've talked to the teachers, and they say he can make up the work over Christmas so they're going to give him C's to get him through fall semester."

"Are you allowed to advance a grade like that, Todd? What if Bucky decides to not do that work over Christmas?"

"Oh, he knows better than that. He'll make up the work if I have to come in and do it for him myself!" Todd stopped talking and shifted awkwardly in his chair as he realized what he had just said.

"Todd, you might double-check the state athletic association's code of ethics on this, but I'm pretty sure you all can't float a grade for Bucky during the playoffs. Would be much wiser to get him in here, sit him down, and explain to him that he has a lot of makeup work to do now, not later."

"John, here you go again! You've never run a high school, but you are so quick with all the answers! I'll tell you what let's do. Let's call the coaches in here right now, and Bucky's dad, and the football boosters, and all the fans who follow this team every year, supporting it with all kinds of gifts, banquets, paying for the long bus trips. Then, you just tell them that you've decided Bucky can't play. I'm sure they'll all pat you on the back for what a great leader you are!"

"Todd, none of what you just said should have anything to do with this decision. First, let's just call the state athletic association. Did anybody bother to ask if this was OK?"

Todd grabbed the phone, made the call, was told that grades could not be arbitrarily given ahead of time, and that Bucky would have to sit out the playoffs if he was failing fall semester.

"Now, John, you happy? Boy, we've just turned our backs on this whole school, this whole community! Good grief, why didn't you let me handle it? I had it all worked out. I had it fixed, John!"

"Yes, you did indeed have it fixed, Todd. What might have happened later if another school turned you in might have led to you being suspended as principal of this school by the state board."

"Just leave, John. But before you leave, tell me one thing: What do I tell them all?"

"Tell who?"

"All the rabid dogs that are fanatical loons over this football team."

"Well, I'd ask the state athletic association to fax you a letter advising you what Bucky needs to do to regain eligibility for any of the remaining games this fall. Then, I'd call Bucky and the head coach in here, and I'd explain to them that you are sure glad you double-checked this, 'cause it saved Bucky and the whole town a lot of embarrassment later on . . . by the way, Todd, I'm proud of you."

"Proud of me? For turning my head the other way all fall while Bucky got himself into this mess?"

"No. Proud of you for doing the right thing."

"It sure doesn't feel like I did the right thing, John."

"Oh, being a man of principle is not about feelings, Todd. But I promise you, later this winter—long after football season is over, and later down through the years when you think back on this moment in time when you and only you had to grit your teeth and pick up that phone—you'll sleep real good at night."

"Oh, John, give me a break! I won't get any sleep for several days. My phone will ring off the hook, and the newspaper will be all over this—it will be a nightmare! And you, of all people, Mr. School Culture, should know that this will blow this town sky high."

"Todd, think about what you are saying. One student—for some reason—goofs off all fall and doesn't fulfill his commitments to his school, his teammates, his coaches, his other teachers, and his parents. Yet you were tempted to somehow enable his immature behavior and let him yet again get away with not suffering any consequences. Most likely, for years he's been covered for, been let off the hook, been made to feel that because he can run a football he's somehow better than everybody else."

John raised his voice and kept going. He was tired of Todd burying his head in the sand or making up new rules every time something uncomfortable came along. "Let's say that you would have been able to pull this off. Let's say no one called your hand on this. On graduation night this spring, do you think Bucky Jones would be singing your praises for teaching him situational ethics the way you were planning to do? Do you think he would go on to college and suddenly turn into a model student? Do you think he would have even gone on to play ball in college? I doubt it. I doubt that he'd have made it through fall practice. Why? 'Cause he'd not been taught back in high school about being a man of character. Kids who are allowed to be 'characters' all the way through their childhood don't suddenly become people *of* character when they grow up. You just did Bucky Jones one of the biggest favors anyone's ever done for him. You showed him what being a real man is all about."

As much as he hated to admit it, Todd knew John was right. He stayed true to doing the right thing and handled the matter with integrity, instead of trying to "fix it" with his own set of ethics. And in the next few days, he was shocked that the entire community stood up in his defense. Soon several other students with failing grades were suspended from various extracurricular clubs around the building because teachers came forward with a new hope that the policies of the school would indeed be enforced. And Todd began sleeping better than he had in years.

* * *

In Talent Is Never Enough, *John Maxwell (2007) reminds us that talent is only part of the equation. To reach full potential, one must cultivate the other variables—including character, relationships, courage, and responsibility.*

SUMMARY

As the semester winds down, Todd finds himself in a dilemma, as his star football player has not kept his grades where they need to be for him to participate in the playoffs. Todd looks for a way out, but John reminds him that situational ethics is not the way to go, nor will it teach the student what he needs to be a productive citizen later in life. Despite fearing the wrath of the entire town, Todd does the right thing.

Chapter Eleven

Peer Harassment (The Unspoken Subculture)

She cried herself to sleep, scared of what the dawn would bring. And no one seemed to notice, as day after day, the torment continued just beneath the surface, just beneath the murmur of those who pretended everything was OK.

Todd's phone call woke John in the middle of the night. "Todd, it's one A.M.! What's wrong?"

"Just got a call from a frantic mom, John. Need you to meet me at the office first thing in the morning if you can possibly make it."

"I'll be there."

John drove through the December darkness, remembering the years of predawn drives he himself had made to be at school early and ready to handle any situation that might be a part of that day. This life of leading a school was not one for those who could not daily look the stress of serious human issues in the face. Todd met him out front, where buses were already unloading students.

"John, I have a mother coming in about ten minutes, and I wanted you to hear her story firsthand. I don't know what to do, and I just thought maybe you would have a solution."

"Well, can you give me a clue? How bad is it?"

"I've got a death threat on my hands. I just had no idea."

"Have you called the police?"

"Yes, but the mom made me promise to let her come in first and tell me what she could. She's a nervous wreck."

"OK. But Todd, you've got to really listen to her, take notes, don't make any promises, don't share any info about other students. You've got to handle this so carefully."

"I will, John. I promise."

When the little mother sat down in Todd's office, she was shaking all over, and it was evident she had been crying and sobbing all night.

"Mrs. Brown, just tell us what happened. I'm going to take notes, and then we'll make sure the police help you as soon as they get here. It's going to be OK." Todd was cool, mature, reassuring. John had never seen him in this light before. He was pleasantly surprised.

"Well, I had known for about two months that something was bothering Callie. Her grades had dropped, and she was tense around the house. She'd even lost weight. And she started making up all kinds of reasons for not going to school."

"Did she indicate to you what might be the problem?"

"No. And when I tried to get her to open up, she'd just change the subject. I thought it might be boyfriend issues or just typical teenage depression that they all seem to go through. Then, last evening, I noticed her pacing back and forth after supper and looking out the window. I had finally had all I could take, so I just asked her: 'Callie, who are you afraid of?' That's when she just burst out crying, and yelled: 'Momma, he's going to kill me!'"

"Did she give you a name? Was it in any way related to school?" Todd tried to remain calm, but he was himself now shaking as he tried to write all of this down.

"Yes, she finally told me that Jimmy Bates had been teasing her all fall. First it was a game, just like he had done with all kinds of girls for years—since he was in middle school. But Callie made the mistake of setting him straight one day in front of some of his friends, and from that point on, it just escalated out of control."

"Well, be assured, Mrs. Brown. We will get to the bottom of this, and Callie will not have to be afraid anymore. I am so proud of her *and* you for coming forward like this. The police will be here any minute, and they will guide you through what needs to be done next."

Todd had deep compassion for this mother, and John could tell that he was enraged that this harassment had gone on in his school. Later, after the police had taken a statement and explained to Mrs. Brown about how restraining orders work, he and John sat alone in the office. For a long time, Todd just stared at the wall.

"John, I am not going to allow this type of nonsense to go on in this school! Tell me what to do!"

"Well, for starters, you've got to assume that this may not be the whole story. Wonder if Jimmy's made it to school yet? Might want to talk to him one on one while you're waiting for the police to get back here to interview him."

"I want you in here too, John, as a witness."

"I'm right here."

As soon as Jimmy Bates strutted into the principal's office, John had to not give in to the temptation to light into the young man with a verbal lashing. Jimmy had a smirk on his face and had a gang of friends waiting outside for him who apparently obeyed his orders.

"Jimmy, I need you to tell me what's going on with Callie Brown. Her mother is so upset she's talked to the law this morning about your harassment of her daughter."

"I ain't done nuthin' to Callie. I can't help it 'cause she can't handle a little rough talk every now and then. Who she think she is, somebody special?"

"Rough talk? What kind of rough talk?"

"Just me and the boys playin' around. Nobody got hurt."

"Well, Jim, here's the deal. You're in big trouble. And possibly, you won't be coming back to this school for a long, long time, *if ever*. Because I'm not putting up with your trash talk anymore, especially if you're out here on school property threatening other students."

"Why you pickin' on me, Mr. Principal Man? It ain't just me who's doing some talkin'. There's a whole lot of trashin' going down that you and the teachers don't even know about. You all just sort of pretend we're all mindin' our own business everyday, nobody sayin' anything bad to nobody. Guess what? We got a gang started here, man, and we ain't scared of you, your assistant bosses, or anyone else."

Just as Todd stood up, and stepped toward Jimmy, the police tapped on the side door to his office. Within minutes, they had taken Jimmy downtown.

"John, he's right. We all just pretend everything's OK all the time around here, when deep down, we suspect there's a subculture of kids bullying other kids. But we don't have enough guts or time to do anything about it!"

"But maybe, Todd, this is the wake up call that will help you get the staff to face the realities and put a stop to anything that's causing any student to be scared of this place."

Todd looked out the window for what seemed like several minutes. "You know, the students tried to tell us in their interviews this fall. Students harassing other students was mentioned as an issue. I'm going to meet with the entire staff after school today, and before we're done, we're going to come up with a plan to expose the bullies. It will take the entire staff working together on this all over the building, but perhaps a death threat is enough to get their attention."

"Perhaps there are other schools who have turned it around too, Todd."

"Maybe. And if so, we'll find them, and let them teach us. By second semester, I want absolutely zero tolerance in this building for any form of student harassment."

"What will that mean for the gang Jimmy claims is already operating in this school?"

"Doesn't matter who it is, John. If they want to go to this school, they'll grow up and learn some respect. If they can't handle that, they're not going here. Maybe they'll find things more suitable at the county alternative school. Think the super will back me on this?"

"Oh yes, most definitely, Todd. He and the board are serious about rooting out the cancers in this district and building model schools that are the best in the state. Keep him posted, and he'll back you all the way."

"This one's for Callie, John."

"And the many Callie's we don't even know."

* * *

In The Top Ten Mistakes Leaders Make, *Hans Finzel (1994) points to failure to see the true corporate culture as a common weakness of many leaders of organizations.*

SUMMARY

Todd is jolted to the reality regarding the subculture of his school when a mother calls him in the middle of the night after a death threat on her daughter's life. But, he does not attempt to avoid the issue. He confronts the perpetrator, one of his male students, and takes steps to develop a plan with his staff to eradicate from Blue Creek High School the cancer of students bullying or harassing other students.

Chapter Twelve

Modeling—Leading by Doing

The movement died quickly when the leader said the right things, but could not find a way to give his heart to the cause.

Christmas was fast approaching, and John had planned to drop in on Todd for one more visit to wrap up the fall semester. When he walked into Blue Creek's lobby, he was overcome with the ambiance of the school. Everywhere he looked there were signs of the season, and students were obviously excited about something new in the air.

"Todd, what on earth is going on around here? I have never seen this place so full of laughter and this mood of 'doing'!"

"Oh, we're for sure 'doing,' John. The 'dream' team wanted to close out the fall term with something different this year; something that would get the entire student body engaged as never before. So, this is 'Giving Week.' Every homeroom is being extended extra time to work on a project that will give back to the community in some way. It started out as a simple idea that I thought was manageable, and it just keeps growing and growing."

"Well, I can just say this: I've never seen your school look so much like a fun place to be. And the student art projects on the walls, the music being played in the hallways—the staff even seems to be getting into it."

"Oh *everybody's* into it. I've never seen this bunch of kids so excited about anything—not even the prom!"

"Does it go on all week?"

"Yes, it ends on the last day as we go into Christmas break. Basically, when the kids leave this Friday, they will flood the town and community with hundreds of gifts of kindness—from food baskets given to the shut-ins, to toys for the daycare centers, to clothes donated to the non-profits in town, to kids caroling at the local senior citizen centers—Blue Creek will literally paint the town with goodness."

"I'm impressed, Todd. And may I ask, what will you be doing to be a part of this Friday blitz of the community?"

"Well, I won't get to be here, John. I'd already planned on leaving Thursday night for an out-of-town hoops tournament with some buddies from college. We do this every year, and this time the tourney has two of the top college teams in the country squaring off Friday afternoon."

"Oh, too bad. Well, perhaps next year. I'd say this will be an annual event for your school now. The town folk will absolutely love this and will be so appreciative."

"I know. The local newspaper already wants to do a story. They called this morning and want to feature me talking to the student body Friday as we wrap up the project and send the kids out into the community with their gifts."

"Wow! What a way to capture the whole school being unified for a great cause. Who's going to fill in for you, Todd?"

"Probably no one. I just told the paper I'd not be available, but we'd think about it next time."

"Todd? You turned down the paper getting to be a part of this?"

"Yeah, we're not about all the hype and praise. Just about the kids learning more about the spirit of the season."

"Aren't you missing the point a little here?"

"What do you mean, John?"

"Well, I just mean if the entire student body is all excited over doing something that serves the whole town, and even your staff is helping, this is a rare moment in time when your school is truly a family—not a dysfunctional family; not a family that pits the 'haves' against the 'have nots'; not a family bickering over self-interests. But truly a community of folks working together on a common mission to make life a little better for others. This is a huge breakthrough, Todd, from what you were telling me earlier in the fall about the various issues around here. If I were you, I'd think long and hard about missing this Friday."

"But John, you don't understand. This annual get-together with my college buds only happens once a year. I never miss. They, too, are family."

"But, they will understand something as important as this, Todd. Surely you could show up a half day late this year."

Todd was getting mad, and John could tell he had struck a nerve. "You sound like my wife, John! She said the exact same thing. She even wants me to choose a project for our office staff here, so we can also jump in on the fun."

"Sounds like a great idea to me."

"I knew it would, John. I knew it would. So you really think it would make that much of a difference if I was not around here this Friday?"

"I think you being here Friday, front and center in that gym when you have all the students and the staff in an assembly, and you telling them personally how proud you are of this school—I think it would make a huge, huge difference in how everyone remembers this project, and what you all gain from it long term."

"Well, I could arrange I guess to not leave until Friday right after school. If you think it's that important John, maybe I can work something out. I just never saw myself as having such influence on this school. They have always rolled right along without me on things like this in the past."

"Well, maybe they rolled along, but not as smooth as you had assumed. They need you, Todd. This school needs their leader to be there for them on the good days and the bad. Let them celebrate this magical gesture of love for the community with you—not try to tell you about it later after you get back from your trip."

"You really think they see me as their leader?"

"You *are* their leader, Todd. Blue Creek's CEO is you, with the help of many other leaders in this school and community. But you're the one sitting in the principal's chair. You're the one they so thirst for and to let them know you love them, and you love this school."

Tears rolled down Todd's face as he reached out and shook John's hand, and simply said: "I'll be here Friday."

* * *

In The Transformational Leader, *Noel Tichy and Mary Anne Devanna (1986) carve out a new definition for the leader of the twenty-first century. This leader is looked to as an architect of change, and motivating and inspiring followers to embrace that change makes all the difference.*

SUMMARY

As Blue Creek High School begins to be transformed and the students embark on a huge community project at Christmas, Todd retreats to his former tendencies by planning to miss the day before Christmas break to meet college friends at a basketball tourney out of town. John reminds him of the role he plays in modeling for his students and staff and that he is no longer just a manager, but someone the school community looks to for unselfish leadership.

Chapter Thirteen

Hiring the Best

To build a great team, the leader must find and develop great team members. One does not happen without the other.

John was enjoying a magical Christmas season with his family and was surprised that Todd called him at home while on his holiday break.

"John, I need to talk. Big decisions to make before the start of second semester."

As John walked into the empty school, where only a few days earlier hundreds of students and staff had filled these halls with laughter and an outpouring of love for the community, he thought to himself: "Without the people, this is just another building. Nothing special about this place without the kids, without the staff, and without the human interaction."

"A school is not a building, Todd. A school is people learning and growing together." Todd looked up from his desk, somewhat surprised. He hadn't heard John come in the front door.

"Never thought of it that way, John. Matter of fact, I sort of like it around here when everyone's gone home for a few days. Anyway, thanks for coming down two days before Christmas. I've got a problem."

"I figured you must have or you wouldn't be here working this week." John grinned, and Todd laughed, nodding his head in agreement.

"Oh, normally I'm not near this place this week, but I need to nail something down before the first day of second semester. I have two staff openings as a result of a resignation and a retirement. I am getting some pressure from the community to hire a couple of folks who have subbed for us a lot this year. And it would make things a whole lot easier for me to just go ahead and hire these two. But the super doesn't agree. He wants me to open it up for several days and run an ad in the paper, shop around. You know, make it a big deal as if these were the two most important positions on earth. Now John, I like Dr. Evans and all, and I admire him. But he just doesn't understand this community. When they say they want somebody hired, we'd better listen to them."

"Sounds like you've made up your mind, Todd. What did you need me for?"

"Well, I was hoping you'd talk to the super for me and explain the bind I'm in, and what I want to do to work it out in the best interest of everyone."

"What bind are you in, Todd? Isn't it your decision with input from your school council?"

"Yes, but . . . "

"And, you say you have it worked out in the best interests of everyone. Does that include the kids?"

"What do you mean?"

"Simple question, Todd: Are these two candidates the best teachers you can find for this school?"

"Well, probably not. I guess we could go all out and wait until we have searched all over this half of the state. But that would take weeks and weeks. We need these positions filled by January 3rd."

"What's the rush?"

"'Cause I don't want to have temporaries in here running two of my classrooms as we start second semester, John, while we look for the permanent hires."

"Seems to me because these two you're thinking about hiring have subbed a lot for you this past fall anyway, you do have some flexibility. Hire them to start off the semester, but then keep the search going."

"But, John, people will be upset."

"Who, Todd, will be upset?"

"One who would be is Banker Dotson, who is an uncle to one of the subs I want to hire. He's already called me at home twice and even stopped me to talk about it at the grocery store the other day."

"Who else?"

"Well, the other one they want hired because she's always so good to sub on short notice."

"*They* want hired?"

"The three teachers who run the back hallway. When they get together, it's hard to buck them, John. We had such a great ending to the first semester, I just don't want any grief as soon as they all get back to school."

"So, in a nutshell, you're willing to sacrifice going after the best, to save you some discomfort now."

"No, John, it's not that simple. It's more complicated than that. You know how this game works. People want to have input. That's what I'm doing—I'm listening to suggestions and taking input."

"What does your school council say?"

"They're all fine with whatever I decide. They don't want to be doing a lot of interviews over the break."

"One more question, Todd."

"What's that?"

"I asked it earlier, but I'll ask again. What about the kids?"

"And you mean?"

"If you're not taking the time to go after the best, even if it takes weeks and weeks, who really loses in the long run?"

"The kids? How do they lose? They'll get along fine with these two new teachers. Both of them are popular in the community—just good folk, John."

"Here's what I'd do, Todd. Hire these two as substitutes, but explain to them that you're posting these positions and that it may take several weeks to complete the interview process. Then, you and your council take your time, and do your best to find the two best teachers you can possibly find for this school. Maybe it will be these two subs, or one of them, or maybe they will not be the best applicants after all. But next summer, when you look back, won't you feel better that you didn't rush to a decision over something as crucial as finding the best staff for your school that you can find?"

"OK, OK, John. I'll do it by the book. I just don't see what the big deal is about this!"

"Tell me one thing, Todd."

"What?"

"If this were a football or basketball coaching position, how would you handle it?"

"I'd go after the best I could possibly find, even if we had to help move them here from another state."

"Then there's your answer. You want to build a great school, don't settle for anything less than great teachers. Start setting the same expectations for your teacher hires as you do for your coaching positions. It will make all the difference."

"A great team is made up of great players, developed by great coaches."

"Exactly. And your team, Todd, is not the football team, the basketball team, or any other of your sports around here. Your team is your faculty. Your coaches are part of that faculty. Develop a great faculty, and you are on your way to having a great school."

"Do you see me, John, *ever,* being a great coach for this great faculty team you dream of for Blue Creek?"

"I think it's very, very possible Todd—if you want it bad enough."

* * *

In Professional Learning Communities at Work, *Richard DuFour and Robert Eaker (1998) challenge the educational community to build and develop teacher teams in ways that transform schools, emphasizing that a student-centered professional staff is the key to an effective school. Their formula is based on the premise that teachers analyzing student work together and in an ongoing manner, and then making the needed adjustments, leads to huge improvements in student success and achievement.*

SUMMARY

Todd is tempted to yield to a path of least resistance when hiring two teachers to start second semester. But John asks him to think about the long-term effects if he is not truly going after the best two candidates for the job. John compares these decisions to finding the top coaches for the football team. Todd admits that in that situation he would try hard to find the best in the state and realizes he needs to adopt the same philosophy in building his entire staff at Blue Creek.

Chapter Fourteen

Seniors—Prepared for Life?

They come to us as babies, and they often leave us too soon—far from ready for what awaits them on the other side of the door. And we'll see them no more, these children we've taken care of day by day from the time they were four years old.

January was here, and John could tell Todd was overstressed as the pressures of second semester were already on him.

"I've got kids lined up outside the counselor's door, John, suddenly wanting to apply for college scholarships. They should have been working on these months ago, even last year."

"I hear similar frustrations from parents of high schoolers at my church. Do you think it's just a case of the kids not really being ready to think about such big decisions, or is it something broken in the system?"

"I think it's both. But something's got to change, 'cause we have several graduates every year who end up not going on to school, who we had assumed would be ready for college."

"What do your counselors say?"

"That's just it, John. They are so swamped with everything we pile on them these days, they just tread water and hope they can make it to graduation in one piece. I do know they meet with the upperclassmen early on, well before their senior year. And they provide them with all kinds of materials that should get them thinking about furthering their education after high school. And we really stress taking the practice

ACT early around here, so both the students and their parents will have some idea of what type of school they should be zeroing in on, and what colleges will be expecting as entrance criteria."

"But it's still not enough, is it?"

"No, not even close. I see kids out at the golf course every summer or at ballgames in the fall that I know have no business fooling around and not going on to school. I am amazed that they seem to have no clue that their future employment potential will be severely limited if they don't have some type of specialized postsecondary training."

"Do many of your kids join the service?"

"A few. But again, even some of these don't seem to think it through."

"Todd, your frustration is shared by many others in this community, and our superintendent is for sure wondering why we have so few who go on. So many kids at this age make poor decisions that will affect their entire lives. And many just seem to not have the drive or the skills in some cases that they should have attained in all their years in K–12 to go on and keep furthering their education. Let me tell you a quick story."

"Sure. Maybe it'll help me relax. Seems all that rest and getting refueled over the break is already gone."

"My sister's boy, Jake, was the talk of the town all the way through elementary and middle school. He was a smart kid, talented in both music and sports. Everything seemed to come easy for him. Our entire family thought he would for sure go on to college and excel in the career of his choice. But Jake must have thought his high school would do all the work in finding him a scholarship. He was so sure he was going to play college baseball, he dropped out of his music classes and put all of his eggs in one basket. His grades suffered too because he practically lived at the ball field."

John paused, and sadness spread over his face as if talking about his own child. "Well, guess what? Jake pretty much stopped growing by the time he was sixteen. So, yes, he had the best arm of any of the pitchers in the region as a twelve-year-old. But by late high school, he had come back to the pack. He still could pitch, but so could a lot of other kids that he had dominated when in Little League. And the college scouts that everyone told us would come calling? They never came."

"What did your sister do?"

"She and her husband realized too late that Jake needed to be cultivating all of his talents and abilities because most likely he wasn't going through college on a baseball scholarship."

"Did it work out?"

"No, it didn't. Jake had the backing of his family, and there were ways he could have gone right on to school. But he decided if he couldn't play ball, he'd put off college until later. He landed a job at a local factory, got married, now has children of his own, and the last time I talked to him, he was still saying 'some day.'"

"John, I see kids making similar decisions all the time. And often, they don't have the support at home that Jake had."

"That's right. If a kid like Jake can fall through the cracks, how many others don't have a chance with the way our present system is set up?"

"But how can I change it, John? I have this same discussion every year with my counselors, and we seem to never get any further than feeling guilty that as the high school in this community, we're not doing enough."

"How serious are you about this, Todd?"

"John, I, too, have relatives who have thrown away their potential and either not gone on to school or dropped out before getting a degree. If you've got a plan, I'm in."

"Well, I was just thinking. The way your students have jumped on this whole idea of sharing with you what they feel Blue Creek could be doing to truly turn it into a great high school, what if you formed a 'think tank,' made up of community leaders, staff, parents, someone from the district office, and students? What if this 'panel' spent the next few weeks devising a plan that would involve the entire community, with its sole purpose to help these high school kids, from freshmen year on, in preparing for life after their Blue Creek years?"

John stood up and paced back and forth in front of Todd's desk as his passion and excitement caused his voice to raise to a high pitch. "What if every one of your students were required to develop a personal plan? A plan that included visiting a variety of sites in the community so they could learn more about various careers. A plan that navigated them all the way through their high school years, with the goal being that they would be well prepared for their next step in life. Maybe it would indeed be joining the military. Maybe it would be going on to technical school, nursing school, working on a two-year degree at the local community college, or working on a four-year degree.

"But, Todd, not one of them would be left on their own like it appears they are now. And we all wouldn't be blaming your counselors and the kids any more for getting lost in all the college applications and other 'stuff' that seems to overwhelm them to the point they don't know what to do. Instead, we all, I mean the entire community—including parents—would help with this 'life plan,' or whatever you'd call it. And we'd not let one of your students fall through the cracks. Not one."

"So, not only would we steer the Jakes of the world toward fulfilling their potential, but we'd steer the kids who right now maybe don't even have an older family member who has even gone to college."

"Yes, Todd, you're right on target. Can you imagine the difference we could make in the lives of these kids, after they leave Blue Creek and walk into a big ol' world that too often just swallows them up while they're still in their teens."

Todd had a gleam in his eye. "John, let's do it!"

"Let me ask you a question, Todd. Just knowing how people are sometimes, what if some on your staff think this is silly? Maybe they think we should let these kids make their own decisions after they've made it to ninth grade. And maybe a lot of your high school students themselves will resist this plan. Maybe they like goofin' off and coasting, and thinking about getting out of this place without a clue about what's next for them in life."

"Oh, for sure, John, I'll have staff who won't believe there's really that much of a need. And, as always, we'll have kids who will fight us all the way. But, you know what? Our current model is not getting it done, is it? The superintendent's office sent us a report the other day on our graduates and what they're doing after high school. Well, for starters, about thirty percent of our ninth graders aren't even making it to graduation day with their class. They're dropping out. And, only about twenty-five percent of our seniors are going on to complete a college degree! So John, it's time to smell the coffee, and face the truth—we're not an effective high school, are we?"

"Depends on how you define effective, Todd. If the community still sees it as the necessary passage from adolescence to adulthood, with your seniors going to work on the family farm, in the local business community, or for nearby factories, then sure, Blue Creek's doing OK. See, this is what many in my generation did, and it worked fine. But today, that plan no longer meets the needs of the community because it can't employ near all these kids. And number two, the old plan certainly doesn't do justice to this generation of teens. They need to be tapping into their full potential. High school should be a stepping stone, not the final chapter of formal learning."

"John, you know what I need more than anything else, though, to really change the system?"

"What's that?"

"I need the superintendent to help me with the funding to hire more counselors. We just do not have enough staff to truly be working with these kids one on one, and coaching them through their last couple of years of school so they will indeed fill out the college applications, visit campuses, prepare for and take the ACT as often as necessary, sincerely jump into their classes here, and prepare for college—or some other post-secondary training. And, perhaps most important, my counselors need to have the time to be meeting with parents, getting them to take ownership and help with this whole process of walking their kids right to the front door of the next place they need to be in training after high school—wherever that may be."

"Tell you what I'll do, Todd. You put this 'think tank' together as soon as you can. And I'll talk to the super about your staffing needs. I know for sure he will applaud your ideas, and I know he is not happy with allowing the parts of the system that are broken to remain that way. He just may indeed channel some funds your way to pilot something that could change this high school forever."

* * *

In Global Leaders for the 21st Century, *Michael Marquardt and Nancy Berger (2000) share insights from several leaders from a variety of professional backgrounds. These formulas for organizational effectiveness in a fast-paced and changing culture hold clues for school leaders, because many traditional paradigms that have been a part of the schooling system for decades no longer align with the needs of students.*

SUMMARY

January is here, and Todd's counselors are mobbed by seniors wanting assistance in what to do after high school. Todd and John discuss the reality that with the current shortage in human resources, Blue Creek will again come up short in all the graduates being well prepared for their next step in life—some type of postsecondary training. John proposes a bold plan to get the entire community involved in fixing this broken system. Todd realizes how unfair the current model is for a significant number of his students, including the high number of kids that drop out of school along the way, and is himself ready for change.

Chapter Fifteen

Curriculum—If Not Relevant, It Is Useless

Often what a child needs and what we adults force feed him are two different things.

The winter weather brought Todd some snow days—bonus time to work on his "think tank" for getting more Blue Creek kids through high school and more of them on into post-secondary. But, as he and John knew would most likely happen, a major roadblock was thrown up by some veteran teachers who saw no reason to change anything.

"I'm just going to table this, John, and maybe we can work on it this summer."

"Why? I thought you were gung ho about the potential to get more of your students prepared for life after high school."

"Oh, I was. I went home after we talked last time and couldn't sleep that night. For the first time, John, I felt like there was a special reason why I was the principal at this school during this point in time."

"Then if your heart is telling you this is a good thing, listen to it, Todd, and stay the course. I think you're on to something that many other high schools across the state would want to know more about, once Blue Creek pilots it and gets some details worked out."

"But, John, I have several teachers against any such changing of how we do things around here. Not just one or two—but several. And they have some key leaders in the community stirred up too. I just don't have the energy, or maybe it's called courage, to fight these people. I've about decided to not do any changing of anything and just ride the spring out like we always do. The kids who make it, great. The kids who don't, well, as one of my teachers put it: 'It's their fault. They're big boys and girls.'"

"Do you really believe that, Todd?"

"No, I don't. I don't believe teenagers can be held totally responsible for not being ready to graduate from high school or not ready to go on to more school after they leave here. I think we have to do a whole lot more coaching them and guiding them. I think it's a joke how many of our graduating seniors underachieve after they leave Blue Creek."

"Then don't table it, Todd. You know you're on the right track with this."

"John, I'm not going to fight people all spring!"

"Tell me, what don't these teachers who are resisting want changed?"

"To be honest with you, mainly it's the fear of having to give up some of the traditional classes we've offered here for years and years. When the 'think tank' group started looking at schedules, curriculum, and barriers that maybe were not necessary, they realized that we are forcing kids to take courses that they are either not ready for or will not need near as much as others we are not offering."

"So, the old guard doesn't care if the drop out rate is still embarrassingly high, and only a fourth of your graduates are actually getting college degrees, as long as they get to teach the old favorites from a time gone by."

"Exactly."

"What are some examples?"

"Well, John, for starters, we're still into Latin around here. Mind you, our elementary schools in the county are not equipped to teach foreign language, when it really should be introduced at the earlier ages. So, that's part of the problem. But still, here, we worship how we used to do it—regardless if the culture has changed and the needs of our students have changed. Same is true with my English teachers, and the math department is bucking this as well. They won't give an inch. All we wanted to do was create more flexibility for the kids who need something much more customized to meet their needs. We have kids who can't read, and kids who can't do basic math. So obviously, our course model we've used for years is broken. Or our teachers can't teach a lick. It's one or the other."

"Well, I would think putting every student in grades nine through twelve on a specific plan that would prepare them better for succeeding in life after Blue Creek would indeed call for some adjustments in all the departments."

"That's what most of the staff realizes, but we're stuck with those who just don't see it. And, I don't disagree with their logic to a point. But I'm looking at the reality here, John. We're not getting it done. We have way too many students falling through the cracks. I used to not even mind when a kid dropped out of school. I figured that was one less problem for me to deal with. But that's not right, John. We're their lifeline! Who cares if all my seniors can say they've studied this and that, when in reality they don't have the skills to function well in society! I want them studying foreign language and anything else we can offer them that turns them on to learning. But we've got to meet the kids where they're at—not where we think they should be. And ironically, some of these same teachers who are blocking this new approach have the most boring, uninspiring classes in the building, and everyone knows it."

"Do they know the students feel this way about their classes, Todd?"

"Yes, some of them do, and they don't care. It's about them . . . *their* background . . . *their* knowledge . . . *their* favorite lessons to teach."

"Are these veterans using technology in their classrooms and the other tools that these kids enjoy working with while they learn?"

"No, John, several of them don't—not true cutting-edge technology. The students 'sit and get,' which really means many of the kids sit and sleep or daydream—bored out of their minds."

"What do the other teachers say about this wasting in the classroom? 'Cause that's what it is, Todd. No matter how much lecturing and spewing forth of knowledge is going on from the teacher, if the kids aren't getting it, if they're not learning—it's wasted time."

"The other teachers don't have much say-so in the matter, John. These people pretty much do it their way, and the rest of us are to fall in line and accept it."

"What about your committees, your teams?"

"Very inactive. I don't push them to meet more because it just causes tension around the building."

"So, in some ways, you have teachers who waltz in here every day, teach exactly what they choose, daring anyone to differ with them, and then they waltz home—sort of like the school district has contracted them to make all the decisions as one would contract a plumber or an electrician to work on a house."

"Never thought of it that way, John, but you've explained it well."

"What if the superintendent were to like this pilot of yours so well, he would come over and speak to your staff one day and outline how he wants your faculty teams working together to iron out every detail?"

"Dr. Evans has never done anything like that here at this school before, John. Wouldn't he be setting himself up for major criticism?"

"All I know is this. When I shared with him what you were working on, he was not only elated, but he's already committed to give you more counseling help this coming fall. I think at the least he'd want to talk to your staff about how your plan has so much potential to turn an average high school into a great high school."

"Would he hang in there with me, John, as the negative forces worked to sabotage our efforts all spring and all summer as we really kicked this into high gear next fall?"

"I think you should make an appointment to go over to his office, and you and he talk out the details. He will be fair to your staff, but he will expect your staff to form into several teams that meet together often to really talk about each student and what support they need to be successful. Not just support for the upperclassmen—but *every* kid in your building. That's what he wants you all doing. He told me it's the only way your plan will work, but that he has seen it work other places, and he and his board are committed to helping you any way you need them to."

"OK, John. I'll go see him. Sounds like we're in too deep to back out now anyway."

* * *

In Teaching with the Brain in Mind, *Eric Jensen (1998) presents a variety of new discoveries and strategies on how to facilitate the learning process so it is much more effective. With a nation of students who as a whole have significant issues with reading for understanding and mastering math, the teacher of the future will need to be much more in tune with the science of the brain and how children learn.*

SUMMARY

Todd meets resistance from his staff as his "think tank" team dives into the gap of why so many Blue Creek High School students are not being prepared effectively for post-secondary and life after high school. Some do not want any changes in the rigid traditional curriculum, feeling that it is up to the students to adjust to the decades' old requirements of Blue Creek. Todd is tempted to give in, but John urges that this is a matter of principle that he cannot ignore any longer if he wants what is best for his students. Todd needs the superintendent to assist and agrees to go see him.

Chapter Sixteen

"Puppy Love" or Obsession?

Mental illness attacks people of all ages, including, too often, our children and youth. When we look the other way, we are dooming our young to a life of misery.

John decided to take Todd out to supper for their next visit. He knew the internal turbulence at Blue Creek from the recent talk of restructure was taking its toll. As they ordered their meals, Todd seemed distracted more than usual.

"Well, I'm curious. How did the superintendent's visit with your staff go?"

"Piece of cake, John. I was surprised at how assertive he was. He just basically said that he and the board were going to assist in Blue Creek High School reversing the drop out rate in a major way and significantly increasing the number of students each year who go on to post-secondary and do well. And he's not talking about some improvement. He's talking about a huge jump in our success rate. I guess we struck a nerve with him when he took a closer look at our data, and this is becoming his pet project, not just an idea our school was considering.

"I'm sure some staff resent him getting so involved, but you know John, the numbers don't lie. It took a lot of courage for him to jump on this so quickly, and now, I have no doubt that we will be making lots of positive changes in getting down to the basics of helping *all* of our kids be prepared for their next step in life by the time they graduate from Blue Creek."

"Wow. Talk about backing from the top! Makes all the difference, Todd. Just follow the plan—support the new staff teams and help them by finding planning time for them any way you can. And the key will be getting the community on board, too. That will make all the difference."

"Oh, I know. They're already calling. And the paper's calling, too. They want to do a big story on all of this. My teachers who were negative and tried to stop this dead in its tracks might as well move on to another school or retire if they're not going to buy into this restructure. It's taken on a mind all its own. And you know what, John? Even though it's already February, I think that even this year we'll see more of our graduating class going on to school next year. Once we laid the real truth out on the table, it was just as clear as clear can be. We can do a whole lot better in helping these kids make wise decisions as they leave here. I'll be honest, it's the best thing we've ever tackled. I've never felt more committed to anything since I became a principal."

"That must explain it then."

"What's that?"

"Well, I thought you seemed a little distracted today. Glad to know it's nervous energy of the good kind."

"Well, yes and no, John. I've got a female student with a personal issue that really has me concerned. I've racked my brain and don't know what to do."

"What's she done?"

"Not so much what, but *how often*, and who she's doing it to."

"Tell me about it. I'll be quiet and listen."

"Well, John, I guess it happens all the time, but a case like this has never been brought to me before. Maybe in the past I was so out of touch the counselors didn't bother. Anyway, we have a sophomore girl who is so obsessive it borders on psych ward stuff. First she was driving her friends crazy with endless e-mails, and letters, and soap opera stories—day after day after day. But now, she's hung up over one of our senior boys and is just about to cause him to transfer to another school."

"Are your counselors working with her?"

"A little—as much as she will let them. But now her parents are involved, and they are in denial that she has emotional issues. So, we're walking a tightrope every day. But if she keeps hounding this guy, something bad is going to happen. I can just feel it."

"What type of intervention program do you all have in place for kids who show signs of struggling with mental or emotional issues?"

"What do you mean, John?"

"I mean, surely this little girl's not the only student in your high school that suffers from some type of mental health issue. Most schools these days are linked up with the local mental health professionals, and references are worked out, fees paid, things like that—so the kids can be assisted with their personal struggles."

"You mean if a student is chronically depressed?"

"Yes, but not just treatment for depression. The mental health field has come so far in recent years in helping individuals of all ages come to grips with various conditions that aren't healthy. There's most likely a significant number of your students here at Blue Creek who are living in an internal nightmare of some kind or another. What type of quality support system do your counselors have in place?"

"John, I'll be honest with you. Except for walk-in sessions when the student takes the initiative, my counselors don't even have enough time on their schedules to assist me with the kids we suspect have alcohol addictions or alcohol abuse issues."

"So, it's pretty much everyone on their own?"

"And that's true for staff, too. I know I have at least a couple of staff who are struggling with depression or chronic fatigue that is work-related. But, I doubt they could ever find our counselors free enough to spend a few minutes with them—even after school."

"Boy, we sure have saddled you folks in secondary ed with a dilemma, haven't we? Give you hundreds of teenagers, not near enough staff, and expect you to pull rabbits out of the hat every day. Talk about a broken system!"

"Now John, don't misunderstand me. Our social agencies are always ready to assist, and they drop off literature every year for our kids. And they help with our annual health fair, too. It's not like my counselors aren't doing everything they know to do with the time and resources we have given them."

"I know, Todd. No one's blaming anyone here. But the system here at Blue Creek, and in many other schools all over the state and country, well, to be frank, it's embarrassing how we have allowed bureaucracy and red tape to keep us from using common sense. So you are pretty sure you have several kids who are abusing alcohol?"

Chapter Sixteen

"Oh, sure—definitely. Some drug abuse, too. Many of them underclassmen."

"Anyone have time to alert their parents?"

"Well, we send the health department literature home to parents, too, John. And we sure try to chaperone our evening and weekend activities here the best we can. Plus, all staff have built into their daily schedules a rotation that has the hallways and bathrooms, even our recreation and outside space monitored closely all day long so the students aren't left on their own to get into mischief. But we can't go home with them. They tend to do a lot of this stuff in the down time when they're not at home or school."

"If you could ask the school board for anything right now, Todd, to provide relief to your overworked staff and to your students who are struggling with personal addiction and abuse issues, what would it be?"

"If I could ask for anything?"

"Anything."

"I'd ask Dr. Evans for what he's already working on—more trained professionals for my counseling department."

"What if you were given the funding to hire a specialist in addictive and self-destructive behavior?"

"Sure, we'd go for it. We'd hire that person tomorrow. I'd even find an extra office around here somewhere."

"Would your staff do their part and work with this person in developing an addition to the school-wide curriculum that focused on Blue Creek being a model school for mental health support?"

"John, earlier this year, I'd have said 'no.' But right now, with the super so intense about us reinventing this place, if he can find the money, I'd say we'd have no problem building what you're talking about into our new structure around here by this fall."

"Well, let's set up another meeting with him then, Todd. You're on a roll, don't stop now!"

"But, John, in the meantime, what about my little sophomore who has flipped out—obsessed over this senior and doing all kinds of weird things?"

"Plus, Todd, what about the many other kids at Blue Creek who are right now struggling with depression, addictions of various kinds, or with suicidal thoughts all bottled up inside?"

"And what about the alcohol abuse? I know it's an issue for several kids in our school."

"You mentioned a health fair, Todd. When do you all do this every year?"

"Usually we set aside a day sometime in April."

"What if, this year, you increased the health fair to two or three days and made that whole week a school-wide project to draw attention to what so many of these kids have no idea how to even talk about, much less go seek out help for. Bring in anybody you can schedule who is an expert in any of these things we've been discussing and turn them loose in the classrooms talking to kids about the danger signs and how and where they can get help. Why should Blue Creek tolerate the toxic ills of the culture as if powerless to do anything about it? Why should this school stay in denial one more day? You've got kids spiraling out of control, and some may not make it, Todd. If we can prevent even just one drug overdose, one drunk driving accident, one student from living one more month in the prison of mental illness—then all the extra effort will be worth it."

"I bet I know what you're going to ask me to do next, John."

"What?"

"Put together a planning team."

"Hey, Todd, great idea!"

"And, John, we never did determine what to do about my sophomore who's obsessing over this boy in front of the whole school every day?"

"Parent conference, first thing in the morning. Her parents need to be told the truth. If this boy is so uncomfortable over this that he's thinking about changing schools, basically, he's being harassed. Some think it's cute. It's not cute. It compares to stalking, and it apparently goes on in our schools all over the country every day, and no one seems to know how to stop it. Well, at Blue Creek, just don't tolerate it anymore. The kids know better, but somebody's got to hold them accountable."

"I agree, John. It is embarrassing, and I'm not going to turn my head and ignore it like I used to do. It's time for Blue Creek to adopt a zero tolerance policy for any behavior, by any student, or adult for that matter, that makes others feel threatened or intimidated. Surely we as a staff of trained professionals have enough intelligence and guts to create and supervise a school culture that is safe and pleasant for all students entrusted to our care."

* * *

In What's Worth Fighting for in the Principalship, *Michael Fullan (1997) outlines a school change model that is practical and doable, taking into consideration the overwhelming and sometimes unreasonable task we have given our principals of this generation.*

SUMMARY

A young student shows evidence of being obsessed with a senior, leading to what Todd feels is harassment. As he and John discuss the extent of mental, emotional, and addiction issues at Blue Creek, Todd decides it is time to put together a planning team to address the dysfunction many students are dealing with in their personal lives.

Chapter Seventeen

Cheerleaders

Supporting our students and worshipping them are two different things.

March was here, and basketball playoffs were in full swing. John expected this to be a short visit, with Todd distracted with postseason tournaments. Instead, Todd had a different issue on his mind.

"John, they're killing me. Absolutely driving me crazy."

"Who, your ballplayers?"

"No, our cheerleaders."

"Uh-oh, let me guess. Their parents want you to pay for a spring trip to Florida."

"How'd you know?"

"Oh, I just remember when I was a principal this came up every year in our leadership meetings with the superintendent. The middle and high school principals were always out there on a limb, trying to finish the season without a big controversy breaking out. Almost always, it seemed the cheerleaders were involved. And almost always, lots of money was being raised for long, expensive trips. How you gonna handle it?"

"Well, it's not just the trip. We've got two or three issues going on here. For starters, I've gotten several phone calls this spring from other parents and members of the community who feel the cheerleader routines are just not appropriate for games that are often outings for the entire family. And I've got to admit—they have a good point. It's not just cheering for the team and getting the crowd all fired up during timeouts anymore, John. The outfits, the type of dances—well, our girls resemble the Dallas Cowboy Cheerleaders more every year."

"Don't you have some type of policy or dress code you can fall back on?"

"No, but that's going to be addressed at our next school council meeting. But I'm tellin' you, the cheerleader coach will fight me on this every inch of the way. She sees nothing wrong with the routines and has already gotten the parents of our cheerleaders all worked up and threatening to pull their girls off the team and take them to another school."

"So they're asking for a huge amount of money for an extravagant trip, they're insulting some in the community with their routines and attire, and what else?"

"They want all kinds of special privileges around here, and the other students are resenting it more every year. They want to leave early for games, they want to come in late on the mornings after games, and they want excuses from class for this and that. They don't just want to be recognized at our spring athletic banquet, they want their own banquet. And ironically, their own parents get tired of how the program gets ridiculously more complicated and time consuming every year. They're the ones who are really being asked to shell out hundreds of dollars. The cheerleaders do all kinds of fundraisers, but you know how that works—their parents are expected to raise or donate a big part of this money. John, it just never ends."

"What do your other club sponsors say?"

"They too are getting so tired of it. At the request of the students back in the fall, we are expanding our extracurricular opportunities. The kids love it, and the participation has been way up this spring semester. But it's getting harder and harder to find faculty sponsors because of the special treatment it appears the cheerleaders get. And to be fair, it's not just the cheerleaders. Our football and basketball teams are given special perks that athletes on other sports don't receive. But, we've always justified that because the two major sports generate so much revenue for us."

"Oh, I know. The crowds pour in for basketball and football games. It's a 'happening' for sure, and having teams to follow is indeed important to the community. But I'm just uneasy with the whole 'class' system thing, Todd. We in education sure have allowed some hard-to-explain rituals to take hold over the years. And as each generation of kids comes along, some of the revered traditions don't hold water anymore. They're outdated philosophies, useful in a previous era, long before this current day when the overall benefit for young people of our sports-crazed culture is being questioned more and more by the masses."

John knew he was addressing a sensitive area for Todd, who had grown up with varsity sports being a major part of his life. But he continued. "This is one key reason why you're wise to grow your intramural program, Todd. Kids will always want to participate in sports. But the community recreational leagues, and school intramurals and club sports are becoming more and more popular, as parents and their children alike are not as impressed with the varsity programs as they used to be."

Surprisingly, Todd did not disagree. "Well, bottom line, John, what do I do about all of this? I can't look the other way anymore. You know how much I love athletics, but I can't allow our student athletes to be treated as a higher class of citizen in this school."

"Doesn't the athletic booster's club play a major role in raising the funds for your athletic program?"

"Yes, and they encourage all our teams, regardless of size, to start their own booster club as well. Most of them have done this and it works well. But obviously, none of these other support clubs are expected to send their teams on trips that cost thousands of dollars. We want our programs to excel, but not become extravagant to a degree that can't even be justified. I've thought about going to the next booster meeting and explaining that we need to be expanding our financial support to all our teams here as much as possible and start putting limits on the extra stuff that a couple of the programs just add to and add to every year."

"Sounds like your next step, Todd. And remember, your school council has every right, and actually, an obligation to be looking at these types of issues carefully, and then adopting policies that are healthy and that support and protect all of the various clubs and teams in this school. It's not the 1950s anymore. Today, there are dozens of student extracurricular and cocurricular groups, which is wonderful. In fact, the long trips are not necessarily the issue. They are a great experience for the kids. But if allowable in the school's policy manual, yet only the same two or three groups go every year and the other ninety percent don't get to go—that's an equity issue that needs to be addressed."

"I remember turning down a tennis team request to go observe a college tennis tournament because we didn't have the money. And I remember telling the choir a trip to New York was a stretch this year, but maybe next year we'd think about it. For the seniors in the choir, next year will be too late, won't it? Not fair to those kids, John. Many of them work just as hard for their extracurricular clubs and teams as anybody else at Blue Creek."

"Just remember, Todd, we should not be in the business of somehow allowing a pecking order to be a part of the school culture. That's the toxin that so easily seeps into the school's tradition, causing some kids to feel cheated. Maybe it's mainly as a result of finances, but still, when it happens, we adults have failed."

* * *

In Asking the Right Questions, *Edie Holcomb (1996) poses five simple questions that allow any organization to navigate the maze of how to improve and how to realize the results it is looking for. Too often, the process of decision making and setting principle-driven goals for schools gets stuck in what is popular—not what is right.*

SUMMARY

The presence of double standards in Blue Creek's extracurricular program raises its ugly head as Todd deals with cheerleader requests for more and more perks. He decides to discuss the issue with his booster's club when he realizes Blue Creek is undersupporting other clubs and student groups.

Chapter Eighteen

Narcissism

Leadership is about being a trusted role model and serving. It is not about controlling, making up a different set of rules, and stepping all over people if that is what it takes to get to the top.

John was startled by Todd's call. He had just been to see him a couple of days earlier.

"Let's go find us a farm pond and do some bass fishing, John. Are you free this evening?"

"I'll make it work. See you after school."

Todd talked nonstop from the time John got in the car, until they pulled up at a beautiful pond tucked back in the woods several miles from town.

"You won't believe it, John. No one could make this stuff up. I did talk to my athletic booster officers, and they are in full agreement that it's time we took a fresh look at how we are funding all of our teams and to explore if there are some smarter ways to handle the many needs of our student athletes. And I already have the whole issue of the need for more policies for all of our extracurricular and cocurricular teams and clubs on the agenda of our next school council meeting. But you won't believe who's been my biggest roadblock the last couple of days."

"Maybe one of your coaches?"

"The chair of our school council, Mr. Packard."

"Isn't he your band director?"

"Yes, and I thought he'd be thrilled to hear we're going to be addressing equity because in the past he's made a lot of noise about how his program needed more support. And I have agreed with him, and we've increased his program's funding every year I've been here. So, I just assumed he'd be ecstatic. But it's been quite the opposite."

"I'm a little confused too, Todd. Isn't what you all are getting ready to address most likely going to benefit band, choir, art, drama, creative writing club—all those programs we sometimes treat as second class?"

"Yes, and I can't tell you how many staff are coming up to me and saying it's about time."

"So what's Mr. Packard's issue then?"

"He's a control freak."

"What?"

"John, I've seen this side of him, but never to this degree. I think that he realizes that this will actually bring to the surface so many needs around our building for all our programs, he will not get to monopolize for his 'wish list' anymore. You know, it's easier to get what you want if you are so intimidating that people are more than glad to say 'yes' just to get you to shut up, and also if you're always plugging *your* program, but are not concerned about the others, too."

"Yes, I see your point, Todd. It's not always an advantage for the squeaky wheels when a more equitable democratic system is put in place. Unless they're genuinely concerned for the whole school, they can be unnerved by such a 'spreading of the wealth,' so to speak."

"And that's not all of it, John. I get complaints fairly often about Mr. Packard's attitude—his whole demeanor. He has his own boosters program, too. And more than once he's talked rudely to parents who were volunteering in the concession stand to raise money for the band. Over the years, he's kicked several students out of the band for various violations of his rules—which are very strict, almost unbearable at times from what some of the parents say."

"How does he handle being the chair of your advisory council?"

"Well, he normally does OK. But I think it's because he gets to be in control. We have such laid-back meetings that he's never challenged by anyone."

"Wouldn't be a narcissist would he?"

"John, you've stumped me again. What's a narcissist?"

"Just what you said earlier—a control freak, but not just that. Narcissists tend to feel perfectly justified in making up their own separate set of rules and will often break society's rules without seeing anything wrong with it. Also, they're mean to people and don't even seem to feel guilty over how they hurt others. They are complicated individuals to deal with and are dangerous to have in charge of anything because once they see something a certain way, they are often overbearing and intimidating of others until they get what they want."

"Wow, you've just described Mr. Packard!"

"Todd, I'll be honest with you. You won't ever reach the level you're capable of as a school if these types are running things. There will always be people hurt. There will always be an undercurrent of distrust. And your culture will be ruined. Narcissists are not leaders—they are manipulative controllers who, much like little spoiled five-year-olds, must always, in the end, get their way."

"John, I'd love to have you do some training for us this summer. You would be so good for my staff, just helping all of us to understand more about leadership."

"Well, maybe I'm not the best one to do it, but you're on to something that's critical, Todd. What does your summer professional development schedule look like?"

"Pretty much more of the same so far. You know, stuff that's probably helpful, but so many of the teachers dread it."

"What if this summer you did PD a little differently? What if this summer your PD was based solely on each staff person's most urgent needs?"

"Sort of like what we're working on for our students?"

"Yes, exactly. Individual growth plans. Now I know you all already do these in some form, but I haven't heard you talk about them, so they must not be effective."

"You're right. I'm not sure some staff even get them back out and look at them after our annual evaluation season is over."

"This summer, with Blue Creek restructuring anyway, it would be a great time to take your staff development to an entirely higher level."

"I'll need to check with the district office and see how much freedom they'll give us on this, but I like it so far, John."

"I guarantee you the super will give you all the latitude you need. He would love to get the entire district involved in this level of customized staff training, and your school's overhaul is just the excuse he needs to let you pilot this as well."

"So, we'll do our best to provide each staffer with the most urgent PD they need? If my new teachers need mentors, if my veterans need to visit other schools to observe model programs, if the entire staff needs a good dose of the most current research and how it applies to running a more effective school, the super will let us do all that this summer?"

"Todd, he will be so glad to hear of this request from a school to truly develop effective individualized growth plans for all staff, he'll find a way. I guarantee it."

"So my Ag teachers, home economics, business, physical education, vocational ed—everyone will get to receive the training they need the most to sharpen their skills in their field of expertise?"

"And your FHA and FFA sponsors, other staff who take care of so much of the extra services for kids, if their growth plan says it's a prioritized need—whether it be a conference they'd like to attend, or bringing a consultant in to work with them here at Blue Creek—we'll do our best to work it out, as long as they will apply their new learning in the classroom this fall or in other ways that meet the needs of Blue Creek students."

"John, the staff will absolutely love this once they realize what it means."

"I think they will, too. For too long, Todd, we've forced too much training on our teachers that is planned by those outside the classroom. This is good to a point, but the experts who are making a difference every day with our kids are our teachers. It's time to listen to them more, and support their needs as never before."

"What about me? What do you think my growth plan should look like?"

"What would you truly like to do this summer, Todd, if you had your pick of any professional development in the country?"

"I'd love to visit the top high schools in the country, at least two or three of them, and just pick the brains of the principals of those schools."

"Todd, my boy, I think that can be arranged. Hope you don't mind airports."

* * *

In Overcoming the Dark Side of Leadership, *Gary McIntosh and Samuel Rima, Jr. (1997) face head on the destructive tendencies of leaders with various types of dysfunction. Narcissism is one type of leadership abuse, and it leads to a betrayal of followers and associates because the victim is in denial of the personal addictions of control and changing the rules to fit the situation.*

SUMMARY

As Todd begins to get more comfortable with his new role as a leader who addresses unhealthy issues and embraces change, he runs into an uncooperative bump in the road—his band director. As the chair of the school advisory council, this veteran reveals a controlling nature in trying to block healthy change, prompting Todd and John to discuss the need for revamping of the school's staff professional development model.

Chapter Nineteen

Termination—Calling the Terrorist's Bluff

For an organization to arrive at greatness, the controllers must be reformed, or they must be removed from the ranks they have poisoned for so long.

As John thought back over the year, he was amazed at how much Todd had grown as a leader. He was like a different person altogether. What John had dreaded, he now enjoyed, and looked forward to each and every visit. But nothing could have prepared him for what Todd was considering as he worked on his annual spring evaluations.

"I need to know, John, if I need to let a teacher go, how to go about it."

"Whoa! What brought that on? You've not said anything about a termination this spring. Is this a new teacher that you can't afford in your budget next year?"

"No, nothing like that. We just received our projected budgets for next year a couple of weeks ago, and everything looks fine. But I have a veteran who is not even close to trying to cooperate in helping the rest of us get ready for next year. And, the more I think about it, he's probably hurt his program over the years more than he's helped it grow as a result of his obsessive control and how mean he is to the kids."

"Are you talking about your band director, Mr. Packard?"

"Yes. John, the more I think back to how many times I've defended him when parents have complained about his hatefulness and his overbearing attitude, I am ashamed that I have covered for him so much."

"Well, you indeed have a problem if his abrasive treatment of other people keeps surfacing. Your role as the principal of this school is to protect it from anything that disrupts the daily flow of good, healthy teaching and learning. And that won't happen without all staff working on effective, trusting relationships with each other, with kids, and with parents."

"And John, Mr. Packard's just gone nuts on us as the chair of our advisory council. Everything we are trying to do to make the changes that the super is backing, Mr. Packard is against. It's almost as if he's not wanting our district office to have any say-so in our planning for next year, and he doesn't care if the school or our students are hurt as a result."

"Is he up for reelection to the council next year?"

"No, thank goodness. He put himself back on the ballot, but he did not get near enough votes."

"So, in a few weeks, he's no longer a part of your school council, correct?"

"Right. But John, in these next couple of months, he'll rip this school wide open if we don't stop him. He's trying to block any major changes and is very good at twisting the facts around just enough so that staff are pitted against each other."

"Do you have a consistent trail of documentation over a period of two or three years in his file that shows a pattern of abuse of the system and of other people?"

"What do you mean?"

"You know, his evaluations, notes you've made of parent frustrations, examples of students being dropped from his band program for questionable reasons, student complaints, or repeated disruption of the faculty to always get his way . . . those types of examples that give you some solid proof that he is destructive to this school."

"John, all I have are his evaluations, and due to how well his band does every year in regional competition, they're strong evals. My assistant principals help me with these anyway, and we all three have had the same philosophy on evals—get them over with, write good things about the staff person, and move on. They take forever, and I must admit, I never planned on firing someone when I took this job. Just not my style."

"May not be your style, Todd, but now you can see why you must take the growth plan and evaluation process seriously. Not only so each staff person is improving in being a quality educator each year, but also to protect the school from rogues like Mr. Packard."

"I know, John. I've messed up bad on this one. I have no documentation that will back up what I have observed for a long time now. But I just know he's bad for our school. He's mean to kids. He's rude to parents. And I want him out of here when next school year begins."

"Todd, it's not that simple. He's a tenured teacher, right?"

"Yes, several years in this school district."

"Then he has one of the most protected jobs in the civilized world. Except for embezzled money or clear evidence of immoral behavior, you will not be able to let him go on such short notice. Let me put it this way: His rights are protected more than yours, more than your coaches, more than the superintendent's. Any of you could be put out to pasture if you don't show results—even if you're wonderful role models in the community. But in this case, even if Mr. Packard is the meanest band director in the state, it doesn't sound to me that you have near enough evidence in his file that will allow you to just up and terminate him this summer."

Todd slammed his desk with his hand and kept raising his voice until he was almost yelling: "But what about the kids, John? What about all the complaints I get? What about how he's not doing the job as our school council chair as he should be doing?"

"I agree with you, Todd, and am in your corner all the way on this. I would be trying to solve the problem just as you are. I'm just telling you that you will need to go another route."

"OK. I'm listening. What other route?"

"Well, for starters, for the first time since you've been Mr. Packard's supervisor you need to truly evaluate him, write down the truth, and then work with him on a growth plan for this coming year like he's never seen before."

"But, John, he'll go nuts!"

"But whose fault is that, Todd? You tell me you've never shown him anything but good evaluations. Have you ever confronted him about how many parent complaints you get on his abrasive style?"

"Sort of."

"What do you mean 'sort of'?"

"I've calmly reminded him that parents do hope he will be gentler with the kids."

"I don't mean to hurt your feelings here, Todd, but it sounds to me you've almost been as intimidated by him as your parents are. And what about the student complaints? How many times a year would you guesstimate that band students come to you or another staff person with pleas for rescue from this grumpy middle-aged man who no one will stand up to?"

"Way too many." Todd slumped back in his chair and lowered his head as he fiddled with his pen and then looked away so he wouldn't make eye contact with John.

"Todd, I'm going to tell you something. And I want you to listen. I dreaded working with you this year because I had heard you were a deadbeat principal. And the first time I came here last summer for a visit, I saw nothing to change my mind. You were so anxious to get out on the golf course, you rushed me out of here, and more importantly, you passed off to someone else a parent who really needed to talk to you. You left me with the impression that you were just making time with this job, and deep down you were not committed to this school or its people. But you've changed. I have been amazed at how you've changed! Now, eight months later, you are the key leader here at Blue Creek."

John spoke with a passion that gave Todd goose bumps. "The school's got momentum. The community's excited. You and your staff are thinking harder about what truly is best for high school kids. And you've got courage—courage that has impressed me more than I can say. Last summer I'd have laughed at the thought of sending any of the kids in my family to this school. Today, I'd proudly walk them right in here and introduce you to them as their principal. Why? Because I know you truly are looking out for all of these students here at Blue Creek. You are standing on principles, not on saving your hide. And the captives are being set free. And that's a big part of leadership, Todd—setting the captives free. But last summer, in some ways, you were in the same category as your band director—washed up, but no one had told you yet."

"I know, John, I know." Todd wiped away tears and pulled out his note pad. "Tell me how to begin this project to save my band director from the junk heap."

"First things first. I think you need to have the conversation with him about how he is not modeling unselfish leadership as your school council chair."

"And really, John, he's made things so difficult for all of us on the council, I'm not sure he should finish out the year. We have a policy that we can remove an officer if the majority of the other council members agree that it's appropriate."

"Then talk to him, and let him know how bad it really is in regard to the trust people have lost for him around the building. Give him the opportunity to gracefully resign before you discuss taking this vote with the full council."

"Then what?"

"Then sit down with him, and for most likely the first time in his career, truly work on a totally honest evaluation, followed up with an individual growth plan that addresses his deficiencies. And, if I were you, I'd find a mentor for him as soon as possible. Perhaps a band director from another district who is known as the best of the best, in all areas of his job."

"John, Mr. Packard is so controlling, so used to getting his way. I don't think he'll let me work with him like this."

"If he bucks you on this plan, Todd, which is very fair, then you have every right to schedule a meeting with Mr. Packard and Dr. Evans, and let the super explain to him that if he chooses to not follow the district's evaluation procedures, then he is being insubordinate."

"What does that mean?"

"It means the super then can, and probably will, terminate him at the end of this school year."

* * *

In The First Year as Principal, *Ronald Thorpe (1995) shares a collection of true stories offered by principals, as they share their various examples of facing adversity while doing their best to run a school well and with integrity.*

SUMMARY

Todd surprises John by deciding that his band director's continued disregard for the health of the school warrants termination. John reminds him he has almost no documentation because his earlier philosophy on growth plans and holding all staff accountable has been so weak. John helps Todd develop a plan of intervention that is fair but also draws a line in the sand.

Chapter Twenty

Serving

The leader looked in the mirror and realized he had not been leading at all. He had been pretending, posing, playing the game. He was embarrassed to be called "leader," and from that day, finally figured out that to really lead he would have to serve.

Late spring was in full swing, and Blue Creek High School was a flurry of end-of-year activities. Todd's plate was extra full, and John had planned on dropping by for five minutes just to say "hi," then not getting in Todd's way until the end of the school year. But Todd would hear nothing of it and asked John to walk around the building with him.

"Oh, by the way, John, I have a resignation on my desk. Seems Mr. Packard has no interest in working with me on his growth plan for next year or in having a one-to-one chat with the superintendent. So, we'll be posting for a new band director soon."

"How do you feel about that, Todd?"

"I feel like we gave him a golden opportunity to improve his effectiveness, while at the same time still staying at this school and in this district. His decision to resign was truly his choice. And in terms of what's best for kids, I'm elated. I want us to find the best band director out there, and I want our music program to soar."

"I'm proud of you, Todd. You handled it so professionally. You were very fair to Mr. Packard, but also looking out for the students and their parents."

"Wanted to show you something, John." Todd changed the subject and was clearly excited about giving John this tour. "See this huge trophy case? For years, it's been here in the front lobby and was exclusively for sports awards our Blue Creek teams have won."

"But I see some band trophies in there, and choir awards, and academic team ribbons—and look, all kinds of trophies from FHA, FFA, drama team. Todd, I had no idea Blue Creek had so many award winners over the years in all of these other areas."

"Yep. I got to thinking over the weekend after all of this stress over our band director. I asked myself what I could do to make sure we treated all our programs as first class. I realized that I had not promoted and supported our other successes as I should have—only sports. That's going to change. I came over here Saturday evening, and rounded up all of these other awards, which were scattered all over the building—some of them stuffed in closets. We're going to have to order another large trophy case, or maybe two, but they're all going right here in the front hall—together."

"Wow. I'm impressed, Todd." Todd didn't say a word. He just took off walking again, with a determined gait John had not seen before.

"I want to introduce you to somebody, John." As they turned the corner, there was a custodian cleaning the back hallway. "This is Mrs. Berry. She's been cleaning this school for fifteen years now. She's our lead custodian. I don't know what we'd do without her. I'm starting a new tradition—the Blue Creek Employee of the Year. Mrs. Berry is our first winner. I announced it on the intercom this morning, and she'll be recognized at our next district board meeting."

"Mrs. Berry, so glad to meet you. Todd certainly had a lot of fine folks to choose from on his staff, so what an honor for you and your entire custodial team." John exchanged a firm handshake, and Mrs. Berry politely nodded, and said "thank you." She seemed to not know what else to say.

"And, to make it extra special, I'm giving Mrs. Berry Friday afternoon off, so she can take her family out to a special dinner, paid for by the school." Todd patted his faithful and hardworking custodian on the back and gave her a gentle smile.

"I've just got one question. Who's taking care of Mrs. Berry's shift this Friday afternoon?" John asked with sincerity as he had no idea what he was about to hear come out of Todd's mouth.

Todd smiled as he looked at Mrs. Berry, and simply said: "I am."

"Want to show you something else." Todd ushered John on down the hall and into the science lab. A class was in session, but when the door opened, the science teacher, a younger woman who didn't look much older than her students, rushed over and gave Todd a big hug. "This little lady has asked for years for us to build her a modern, fully equipped science lab. I've always put her off and put her program at the bottom of the list. I met with the budget team yesterday after school. We're starting with new science equipment this fall—several thousand dollars worth."

"What was different this year, Todd? I mean, all these years and the budget committee had not found the additional funds for this program."

"What was different? . . . Me. I explained why we needed a new science lab, and that we have needed it for a long time, and not one person batted an eye. They all agreed."

"Todd, I'm in shock I think. This is not the same place I walked around last summer."

"Oh, we're not quite through, John. Let's go back to the front office." As they walked, the two men talked and laughed with a mutual trust and respect that is possible only after having vulnerable, honest, and sometimes painful conversations with each other.

Todd put his arm around John's shoulders. "You've changed my career, John. I think I've finally figured it out. It's not about leading by bossing and manipulating everything so I can stay out of hot water. It's about serving. And in serving, there will be hot water. But, that's OK. A leader with some courage can handle it. Even learn to enjoy it if it's making the school better for the kids, the staff, and the community."

"Todd, I am proud to call you friend. I am proud to call you a talented colleague with such vast potential. I am proud to call you a servant leader."

"Now don't start, John. You know how I can get misty eyed every now and then." Todd smiled as they walked back through the front lobby. His office team was in the conference room, going over the details for the rest of the week, and planning the following week. "We learned this from you too, John. We meet, brainstorm, plan, and evaluate everything together. I wouldn't know where to start without this group of people right here."

John looked around the table and nodded with an affirming smile toward Todd's team—his two assistant principals, office manager, secretary, attendance clerk, two counselors, and all the student workers—two for each of the six-period day.

"I wanted them all to get to meet you, John. I wanted to make sure they met my mentor. And I wanted to make sure you met my support team. But I'm changing their name. From now on, they're not called my team. They're Blue Creek's servant leadership team."

John was moved, as he gazed into the eyes of the people who behind the scenes had been helping Todd all year to get this big ship called Blue Creek turned around. "I'm not sure you all know what you mean to your principal and to this school. But I can tell you this—you, as a faithful team, have made a huge difference. This school is on the move as never before, and a lot of the credit goes to Todd and his team."

"No, John, not me. This is my 'rock.' This team has carried this school while I finally learned what it means to serve. I've learned so much from them and from you. So, while I have all of you in the same room at the same time, I just wanted to let you know that this team, including John, is going to be recognized at graduation for your commitment to Blue Creek becoming a great school. I've talked to the superintendent and he loves the idea. In fact, he's going to help with the presentation. So, there's no getting out of it."

Everyone was stunned. "And, to kick off this honor, I want each of you to pick a two-hour block between now and the end of the school year that you would want a break. Give me some time to rearrange my schedule, and I'll cover for each of you on those two-hour blocks. I know it sounds a little crazy, but it's my way of saying 'thank you.' Just promise you'll pick some work that I might be able to do halfway decent for you."

"Well, that settles it," chuckled John. "They'll all play it safe and just give you the task of answering the phone."

"It's a deal," Todd laughed. And his team laughed, too. But not at him—instead with him, with deep admiration and gratitude.

* * *

In Servant Leadership—A Journey into the Nature of Legitimate Power and Greatness, *Robert Greenleaf (1977) outlines what poten-*

tial our society has to truly exude greatness if individual leaders and organizations have their arms wrapped around this principle of living a life of service.

SUMMARY

Todd surprises John by walking him around Blue Creek High School and introducing him to people he is taking the time this spring to honor with his own personal acts of service and gratitude. He begins with the lead custodian, who he has named the school's employee of the year. Todd has become a caring leader and is not the same man who only last summer seemed to disdain the responsibilities of being a principal.

Chapter Twenty-One

Core Values Drive Everything!

The crowd cried for this and that, demanding and often immature. But when the core values of the organization were defined and lived—integrity, vision, and setting the captives free—the lions were tamed, and the storm calmed with a peace that pointed everyone toward a future with endless possibilities.

A week before graduation, Todd's family had John's family over for dinner. The get together had been Todd's idea, and as the evening passed, John saw a peace and humble self-confidence in Todd that made him almost burst inside. He was so proud of his younger partner. As the two sat on the front porch, Todd asked a question he had had on his mind for a long time.

"Will they turn on me, John?"

"What? What do you mean, Todd? Will who turn on you?"

"My staff. The students. Their parents. The community."

"What brought that on? Of course they won't."

"Well, I've just realized as the year comes to a close what we have created for next year. Has all of this just been a honeymoon period because they all were so thrilled to see me show some concern for their school? Now, come August, do I really know what to do over the long haul?"

"Todd, let me put it this way. If you're asking me if it will be easy? I will tell you straight up—no, it won't be. Reinventing and bringing healing to a mediocre or broken organization never is."

"Then, what now, John?"

"Son, you just keep loving people. You just keep letting them know you care. You just keep turning them loose, with all their good ideas, and their hopes and dreams. I love the phrase we've come up with—setting the captives free. Just one day at a time, with your own unique way of leading, set the captives free."

"But what if some of it doesn't work?"

"Todd, sometimes it won't. Sometimes you and your teams will have to go back to the drawing board. But, that's the key. Your teams. Keep them active, keep them thinking, and keep supporting them. Help them stay focused on goals and strategies that are about helping kids succeed and reach their full potential. This mindset of selflessness will solve almost all of your 'nuts and bolts' stuff—the process and structure piece that causes some principals to pull their hair out. Rise above all that. It will be up to you to lead the way in casting a powerful vision for your school—that's your main job. Do it relentlessly, and model it, as I saw you start doing more and more this year. If you will stay with it, others will start casting that vision, too. Soon, the entire community will believe it and help make it come to pass. And Blue Creek will become a better school every year."

"How do you know?"

"'Cause Blue Creek has a solid core values base, Todd."

"Core values base?"

"Yes sir. Now, I'm not sure you all did last year this time. But now, Blue Creek is about people helping people. It's about equity. It's about all the kids. It's about a highly trained staff that works on continuous improvement. It's about good relationships with parents and the community. Those are wonderful core values that will undergird Blue Creek for years to come, even after you've moved on and handed the torch to someone else."

"I ought to write all this down, John. You make us sound like we've figured it out."

"You have. Your staff has. Blue Creek has. Now, when I walk into your school, Todd, I see people who are engaged in good work and fulfilled. I feel the magic of all that talent in those classrooms. I feel respected by the office staff. I see on the walls and down the hallways this celebration of learning and growing together. The culture at Blue Creek is contagious, and it makes me want to be there, right in the middle of it—soaking it all up."

John stood up and pointed across town toward the school. "I now want to go to your football games this fall. And I want to stand and cheer for your band when they march at halftime. And I want to support your academic team by going to its meets, too, and support other student groups as well. I feel so honored that I am a part of your graduation this year. I look forward to working with your staff in the future because they are all so serious now about helping make Blue Creek a great school—a school that has figured out what it means to serve."

"You mentioned culture. Can you really tell that much of a difference?'

"Oh my, Todd. It's like night and day. And that's the magic ingredient. When the culture is addressed, and the toxic issues zeroed in on and the cancers taken care of, the organization can then heal. And when that happens, the battle's won. There ain't no stoppin' Blue Creek now."

"Will you write all this down, John, and come to my next faculty meeting and tell them what's happened?"

"They know son, they know. But I do agree with your idea to get your arms wrapped around your core values. If I were you, at your next school council meeting, I'd start talking about them and I'd refer to them every time you meet and with every team in the school. Even put them on your stationary and talk about them on the intercom and in assemblies with the kids. Help this whole town to believe in and embrace Blue Creek's core values."

"And doing this one thing will make next year all fall into place?"

"You keep the main thing the main thing—never waiver from your principles of goodness and the core values I saw you and your school focus on this year. They're your foundation. Then keep your school organized, and keep your teams working on how to make Blue Creek a more effective school, a school that works 'smart,' a school that embraces serving. If you will do these things first, Todd, you all will figure the technical stuff out day by day, month by month, and Blue Creek can be a top five school."

"Pretty cool. One of the top five schools in the region."

"No, Todd. One of the top five schools in the state. You all will eventually be asked to work with other schools, maybe even in other states and at national conferences. Your model of servant leadership has greatness written all over it. And I don't tell you this so you will be prideful and start being competitive for such accolades. That's not servant leadership. It's not about climbing over others to win the awards and fame. That stuff doesn't even matter. I tell you this so you will realize that you finishing this school year on a high note is not an ending. It's just the beginning."

* * *

In The Servant Leader, *James Autry (2001) shares a practical framework for how a servant leader can build an effective team that leads to growing an effective organization that gets the right results. The philosophy of serving—not directing—has the potential to transform any organization.*

SUMMARY

Todd's family invites John and his family over for supper, and as Todd and John discuss the future, Todd expresses concern that he may not be able to follow through with all the momentum he has helped generate at Blue Creek. John assures him that the key will be staying focused on the core values that he has identified this year. With these as the compass, Blue Creek will remain on the road to greatness.

Chapter Twenty-Two

Passage

Life is full of moments in time, various stages, and rites of passage. And on graduation night, perhaps as no other on this journey down life's road, the high school senior realizes that childhood is over, and adulthood is here. The classmates who've been there every day all these years will go their sorted and separate ways, either into a life of fulfillment and chasing dreams or into a life of never reaching their maximum potential. So when the tears are being shed by parents and faculty on this night of nights, the emotions flow much deeper than the graduates could know. But they will eventually understand—sometimes way too soon.

The month of May is a time of celebration for those in education. Not only does it usher in the magic of summer, but it is a time of paying tribute to the achievements of many over the past nine-and-a-half months. As Todd met John in his office for a quick prayer before he went out in front of hundreds of people to make sure this night was all it was supposed to be for Blue Creek's graduates and their families, he gave his mentor a big, heartfelt hug.

"I'm going to miss your visits, John. Oh my, how I am going to miss them."

"I'm not going anywhere, Todd. In fact, I'll stop by next week before we roll into summer. And the super says you and I have worked so well together, he wants us sharing a lot of what we've discovered this year with the principal's cadre next year. Plus, this coming year, anytime you need to talk, about anything, you just call me."

"Oh, I'm sure I will indeed be doing that from time to time. Well, it's 'game day.' Let's go do it."

John was almost as proud of Todd as if he were his own son as they walked toward the gym together. He knew Todd was feeling the pressure of being the master of ceremonies tonight, but he also knew Todd would do just fine. As the year had unfolded, John had realized that Todd was always able to rise to the occasion when he knew it was crunch time. This night would be no different. But, what Todd did next caught John off guard and was one of the most special things he had ever seen a principal do.

Todd veered off to the cafeteria, where his staff and Blue Creek's senior class were doing final prep. He started at the back, where the seniors were getting in line two by two. And one at a time, he hugged every one. Then he asked them all to give him their attention just for one moment, before the music began to play and they made their final entrance into the gymnasium, which was packed full for this magical evening.

"I just want to say . . ." Todd's voice broke and he had to stop in mid-sentence. Everything was silent for about thirty seconds. "I just want to say to all of you—our dear, precious, talented senior class—thank you. And to our wonderfully talented and hard-working faculty—thank you. This past year, I have allowed all of you to teach me about serving. For the first time in my life, I understand my purpose, my calling, my reason for being a high school principal. Faculty, you have believed that we could be more than an OK school. You've faithfully trusted the dream that we could be a great school. Thus, we are on that road. And seniors, you were the class that somehow got our attention and helped show us the way."

Todd paused for a few seconds, and looked into the eyes of this graduating class. It seemed that only yesterday they had walked into Blue Creek as freshmen—so young, so wide-eyed and intimidated but also eager to be in high school. His voice broke again. Where had the last four years gone? And he still didn't know all their names, a testament to his self-focus for three of those four years that he deeply regretted.

"Those student surveys you filled out back in the fall opened my eyes. From that one simple strategy, when we finally were courageous enough to ask you what we weren't doing as well as we could be, a new school was born. I will always remember this senior class as the students who trusted us, were patient with us, and who helped us in so many different ways to head Blue Creek down this road less traveled—a road called 'serving.' A road that puts our people above anything else—all our people. A road that leads to a true community school. A road that leads to a school that holds not just some of your hands, but all of your hands as we meet your individual needs, and challenge you, and help you in being persons of character, persons of vision, persons who serve and make a difference long after you've left these loving arms of Blue Creek."

The seniors, and the staff, all at the same time stood in unison and gave Todd a long, long standing ovation. Then they all went out and gave the Blue Creek community a night of nights, a graduation service that would be talked about for years to come. And Todd, and his nerves? Todd faced his fears and taught that gymnasium full of people about serving. He called his wife and kids up front and gave his wife a dozen roses for being the quiet strength behind the man. He called John and his family up and gave John's wife a dozen roses and thanked her for loaning her husband to him as his mentor these last ten months.

He called the superintendent up and gave him a plaque from the school, thanking him for believing in Blue Creek and investing in their dreams. He called his custodial and cafeteria teams up and introduced them as the servant leaders behind the scenes who made all the difference. And he called his office staff up, including John, and thanked them for teaching him how to be a servant leader.

And just before he called out every senior's name to come up on stage to receive their diploma, he had fifty students stand. These were what he called Blue Creek's unsung heroes. He then explained that these were the faithful 'servants' who never received the praise, the awards, the trophies—but who were in their classes every day, working hard, and were always such positive role models for the rest of the student body and the faculty. Spontaneously, but almost as if on cue, everyone else in attendance rose to their feet and gave the fifty 'servants' not just a standing ovation, but one that went on and on for three or four minutes.

And the band played, and the choir sang, and Blue Creek said goodbye to its 'children' one last time, then let them go.

*   *   *

In The Fred Factor, *Mark Sanborn (2002) tells the story of what a huge difference one man can make when he commits to being focused on making the lives of others better.*

SUMMARY

Blue Creek High School has a graduation night for the ages, as Todd, for the first time, shows the entire community the 'goodness' factor that has transformed his life in the last year. He models servant leadership by honoring many in attendance who normally would never receive the accolades, including fifty students who had not excelled with awards during their years at Blue Creek, but had excelled in something more — being citizens of character who made the school a better place to be.

Chapter Twenty-Three

Mentor

Too often, we think we have all the answers, when in reality, we know so little that we are not even in the conversation. But if we will stop long enough to listen, and take a good look in the mirror, there just may be a lifeline close by—a mentor and trusted friend who will not just pat us on the back and pretend everything is OK, but who will care enough to help us out of the sea of mediocrity and point us to the road of greatness.

"Last week's graduation was the most powerful, inspiring, moving service I've ever been in, Todd. There were no dry eyes left by the time it was over, and your testimony to what serving is all about did something you may not have intended."

"What's that?"

"You, in such a beautiful and selfless way, cast the vision for this school and community, Todd. Now, they understand. Son, you hit a homerun."

"John, I was so nervous before that service. Oh my, I was sick to my stomach with butterflies. But you know, I just kept reminding myself that that night was not about me, and I had better not let everybody down. So, I just focused on those parents, grandparents, little brothers and sisters, our faculty, and our seniors. After that, I had no choice but to do it right."

"Well, you for sure did it right. People all over town are still talking about it."

"John, I guess this is our last chat for a while—at least for a few weeks. I want to ask you a question. Now that we've tucked this baby to bed so to speak, tell me anything you've not gotten to thus far if you were in my shoes as we start getting ready for this coming school year. And not just this year, but for the rest of my career. I'm not going to say a word—just going to try to take notes like crazy."

"Well, because I've never been a high school principal, I'm not sure I'll be much help to you at this stage, Todd. After the way you've laid the groundwork this year, you'll know what to do."

"John, it wouldn't matter what school, what grade level, what company or business, you will always know how to make an organization better. Your instincts about leadership are unbelievable. I have been amazed all year, especially once I started really listening, at how you can see what others don't see."

"Oh, I think they see it too, Todd. It's just every organization needs someone to move them past the gaps and toxic stuff, and toward solutions. And the solutions will always involve getting back in touch with your people—and putting them first. When an organization truly serves its people that organization has figured it out."

"It seems almost too simple, John. All these years I've thought somehow that I just didn't have what it takes to be the right type of leader for Blue Creek. Then almost over night, as soon as I started working on relationships and truly listening to people—their frustrations *and* their good ideas—everything began to change."

"Because you changed from self-serving and running from anything complicated, to empowering and equipping. Again, you began to set the captives free."

"Setting the captives free. Yes, that is what it's like. Every day, my job is to make life better for others. When I do that, it seems everything else works out fine."

"And Todd, that's your answer for going into this next school year and every year. Don't be scared of all the new work that lies ahead. Remember, in every situation, you're unlocking the door, removing barriers, and empowering people to do what just maybe they didn't think they could do. I've always been amazed at my family doctor. I don't think I've ever been in to see him that he didn't have morning rounds at the hospital and then again evening rounds. But he never rushes me, never makes me feel like he's too busy that day to see me. He has basically given his life to setting the captives free, if we define illness as a prison that holds our bodies hostage."

"Never thought of it that way before, but it's true, John. People I know who spend their time helping others, they don't even see it as work. It's as if they've given up this self-focused notion of 'having it all,' which is so overemphasized in our culture."

"And they seem to have life figured out, don't they? They don't mind decreasing, so others may increase. They don't crave or need all the attention or praise. Instead, their lives are purpose driven. They live on a different level because they are not about themselves, but instead about others."

"This makes me feel so good about this coming school year, John. This 'goodness' factor changes everything."

"Yes it does, Todd. It is a radical way of thinking, of doing, of believing in others, and being driven by noble principles that I am afraid many in our society have gotten away from."

"Well, we're not drifting away from them at this school. But where would you start, John, as I help put things in motion for next year?"

"Just let it be a continuance of this year. Follow through on what was started these last few months—freedom for staff to share ideas with you and each other, effective teams in place and creating new ones as you need to, well-planned individualized growth plans for all staff, working closely with the superintendent on the pilot projects he's investing in here, communication and partnerships with the community as never before so Blue Creek is truly a community school, and more student surveys. And just keep the school's core values and the vision front and center in everything that is done here at Blue Creek."

"Oh, I know. Those student surveys last fall were the catalyst for us realizing we needed to be making some significant changes around here. And I wanted to know more about what the seniors thought about all that we were trying to do this year, John, so I gave each of them another survey before they left here last week."

"Wonderful, Todd! Their feedback will be invaluable. Sometimes an exit interview, or 'one last talk,' sheds light in ways other audits or assessments can't. I guarantee you—your seniors have given you some candid and honest appraisals and perspectives that will go deeper than any other survey you've ever done. There's your starting point for this coming year right there."

"I'm sure they've let us know in great detail what classes and activities we should keep, what we should add, and what we should drop. How would you go about ciphering through all the suggestions from students, staff, parents, and the community?"

"Well, for starters, I learned to actually visualize in my head what a great school would be like if it truly met the needs of every student it served. It's amazing what you then realize is still missing. For example, you can then be honest and real enough to admit to yourself: 'We don't really have the variety of quality math and science instruction going on that we need here at this school. We are not getting it done the way we should. Likewise, we still have students who can't read well. Why is that, and how can we fix it? And no, we don't emphasize the arts enough. What's missing in our art, drama, and music programs? Are there other sports we should be offering? How does our PE program compare to the best in the state? Our vocational program? Our technology?' You see, Todd, most of the time we're conditioned to for some reason make excuses for mediocrity. When we give in to that mindset, we then become numb to that all around us that needs improvement."

"Just tell me, John, in a nutshell, how would you define the school of the future? What could it be if everyone in a community really worked together, and believed in the dream?"

"The school of the future would not be limited to these walls. It would not be limited by time, or bus schedules, or bells, or anything else that has made something so simple and exciting so complicated and uninspiring to many students. My school of the future would be much more about tearing down walls—whatever they might be. Our current system, in many ways, is just the opposite. It has created unnecessary walls—not just for students, but for teachers, parents, the community, even volunteers who want to share their talents with the school.

"My school of the future, Todd, would be like summer camp. This is the best analogy I can think of, and I use it often. My own kids at home have always absolutely loved summer camp. They go, they are immersed in all kinds of new experiences, they learn, they focus on healthy relationships, and they come back home with a smile on their face and with great memories. My kids lost that passion for school while still in elementary. Now why is that? Is it that we herd them in like cattle, shuffle them here and there like robots, mechanically do the same routine day after day after day as if they're working in a factory—

sometimes in large impersonal campus settings that more resemble a correctional facility than a community learning center? Can we afford to stay with a model that continues to be broken?

"At camp, Todd, my kids are there in community with about sixty other kids and ten or fifteen staff. They come home remembering everyone's name. They come home renewed and wanting to explore more about what they learned at camp. Would this formula work for schools? Would churches and other community centers let us use their facilities? Over the last fifty years or so, as a society, have we really thought this through? Have we truly been diligent about the continuous molding and shaping of a service model that is truly what's best for kids?

"See, I think, no let me correct that, I *know* there's a smarter way to educate our children and youth, Todd. Absolutely has to be. Across the land, we still have twenty to thirty percent, depending on what school, of high schoolers who drop out along the way and never make it to graduation day. There's your answer to anyone who is in denial and claiming that we are doing a great job educating our nation's young. *No we're not!*"

"Did you have one thing, John, that you used to sort everything out? A secret formula? I'd love to know your secret formula!"

"I used to use a litmus test, Todd, that helped us so much from year to year, even month to month, in planning and organizing our actual menu of services. I kept a little note in my planner, and I would look at it often. It simply said: 'If it is good for even one child in this school, find the right people to help and stay with it. If it's more about staff, or other adults than it is about kids, be careful—it may actually take you away from the school's core values and vision.'

"Did it actually help you in dealing with the many issues, John? The various positions people take on those issues? The endless fires to put out?"

"Yes, it did. On those lonely days, and as you know Todd, a principal has many of those—when it seemed as though I'd never get to the end of the list of things that needed to be taken care of—I'd read it, I'd say a little prayer, and I'd be OK."

"Just like that?"

"Yes, pretty much. You see, Todd, when you focus on what's best for kids, this complicated mess that we call school turns into common sense, and school returns to its original purpose—which was to simply educate students and prepare them well for life."

"Did you ever share with others that this was your secret for making so many wise and smart decisions all these years, John?"

"Yes. In fact, I read it to the staff on our opening day every fall, and I read it in faculty meetings often."

Todd smiled, grabbed a pen, and scribbled John's quote in the front of his planner.

"And my other rule, Todd, as you know, was to never, ever neglect my family. So, I'm out of here and on my way home to pick my gang up and take them on a trip we've been planning for several weeks."

"Me too, John. I've penciled in more special time for my wife and our kids this summer than ever before. I've never seen them all so excited. And it feels so good, every evening, when I walk in that front door, to hear them say: 'Daddy's home.' And I pinch myself, as I realize: 'Yes, Daddy's home. Daddy's really home.'"

* * *

In Anyway, *Kent Keith (2001) shares paradoxical commandments that go straight to the heart of true servant leadership, as perhaps the greatest of all commandments is illustrated in detail: Serve others as you hope they would serve you.*

SUMMARY

John praises Todd for what an awesome job he did in making graduation so magical for all in attendance. Todd quizzes John about what the model school of the future would look like. John shares timeless tips for how to see the gaps in a school and then envision what it could be if everyone was focused on what is best for kids.

Chapter Twenty-Four

Leadership Cadres

People need people. Professionally, the days of "lone ranger leadership" are long gone. When a small group of educators meet together and discuss the stressors and the strategies that are working well, wonderful healing and growth begins to happen personally and also back in their schools.

John's appointment with Superintendent Evans was delayed for thirty minutes because the superintendent was wrapping up an end-of-year evaluation session with one of his principals.

"Come in, John. I apologize for delaying your morning. I've been meeting one to one with all of my principals this week, and I must tell you, they all have loved the leadership cadre you've facilitated this year."

"Oh, that group's been such a joy to work with, Dr. Evans. I learn more from them than they do from me."

"Actually, John, they say that your insights, probing questions, and listening skills make the group flow so well, they all want to continue it this coming year. I am so pleased."

"Principals need support, Dr. Evans. And in this format, they not only hear some great ideas from the other schools, but they also get to be real, so to speak, and share whatever's on their mind. We've had principals break down and have a good cry while in the shelter of the group. So, not only do we allow time for 'shop talk,' but there is a built in time for getting things off their chests that is therapeutic."

"Tell me, John, has this group been hard to keep on the calendar month to month? I know how principals are always so busy, and sometimes have way too much on their plates."

"No, not at all. Actually, rarely does anyone miss. We rotate where we meet. Sometimes it's here at central office, sometimes it's at a restaurant, and sometimes we'll meet at a school to observe firsthand a new program or project that is working well."

"And you meet for about two hours?"

"Yes, we meet monthly for a morning two-hour session, and I prepare an agenda that includes current leadership research and other items of interest that I share with them. Then we always allow time for success stories from each school. And I referee the venting discussions closely, so we don't get sidetracked into too much griping. We also don't allow gossip. Our goal is to help each other improve as effective, caring leaders. And an added benefit is the participants go back to their schools and feel freer to call each other when needing help on something or needing to send someone to observe an initiative that's working well at another school in the district. So the learning and support that's built in goes far beyond the two-hour sessions."

"Sounds like an effective model, John. And that's why I wanted to meet with you this morning. I wanted to ask you how much time you would have this coming year if we expanded your role. Now, I would still want you mentoring yet another of our principals one to one again. Your work with Marcie and Todd these last two years has been amazing. In fact, Todd's development is my 'feel good' story of the year for this entire district. I just can't believe the difference. When I watched him at that graduation service, I couldn't help but have tears in my eyes. Last year this time, John, I doubted that Todd would be the principal at Blue Creek much longer."

"Todd's a gifted man, Dr. Evans. He just needed someone to take the time to mentor him and help him get beyond himself. Yes, I agree. He's transformed from a careless, selfish manager of a school—mediocre at best, to an inspiring role model for the entire community."

"And I wonder how many more 'Todds' are out there, John? And that brings me back to my question. Would you be willing to help us expand this one to one mentoring model and the leadership cadre?"

"Expand?"

"Yes, take it beyond our district."

Leadership Cadres

"Dr. Evans, two years ago, when I first retired, I would have said 'no.' I did not want to tie up my time with more work down in the trenches. I felt like I had taken my turn, made a difference, and it was time to step away. But working with these younger principals has been one of the most fulfilling projects I've ever been a part of in my life. So, yes, I'm open to expanding the work."

"Fantastic. You've made my day, John. I received a phone call from the state department earlier this week, and they have heard about our principal support project. They want to borrow you for a few days a month to help grow several more principal leadership cadres across the state. And they want you to train a group of retired master principals who they've recruited for one to one mentoring assignments this coming school year."

"Wow, Dr. Evans. I had no idea the word had spread about our mentoring model here."

"Oh yes. Not only have I been telling folks how wonderful it is working when I have the opportunity, but apparently our own principals sing its praises all the time when in regional and state meetings."

"I don't know what to say. This is amazing! But I do not want to get into a massive project that will end up taking me away from my family, my volunteering at church, and my mentoring here for you."

"I've already talked to the state folks about that, John. They are well aware of your commitment to family and a healthy balance in your life. And there's no way I'd let them take you away from the leadership work I need you doing here with our principals. How does fifty days for me in our district and fifty days for the state sound? Would that work?"

"Yes, I can do that type of schedule. But Dr. Evans, I'm going to be honest. Most likely, the principal cadres around the state and the one to one mentoring will grow and grow. What is a fifty-day project now will most likely grow into a full-time job in a year or two. So, I'm a little skeptical about that part of it."

"We've already thought of that too, John. The state's plan is to use our model this year as a pilot. Then, over a two- or three-year period, they hope to add several more trainers like you. Their vision is to grow this initiative so well that soon every principal in the state will be in a small group leadership cadre and will also have a mentor who has been an effective principal."

"What an awesome concept!"

"As is so often the case with the most effective strategies, almost seems too simple doesn't it?"

"Dr. Evans, this will transform this state's entire education system—if the mentors understand and stay with the servant leadership model. It won't work as well if the various cadres start wandering into more vague leadership definitions and sources of advice."

"I know, I know. I've seen your model work, John. It's changing my principals. It's changing this district! I've already had that discussion with the state department too, and they agree. They don't just want any leadership development plan. They want *your* model. That's why they've chosen you to coordinate their pilot. And they won't stop with our state's principals. If this works like I'm confident it will, within three years our model will be out there being used by other states across the country."

"I am in shock, Dr. Evans. Yes, I'll do it."

"You're the best thing that has ever happened to my superintendency, John. Your servant leadership model is contagious. Our district has momentum we've never had before. A lot of that started when the principals you've mentored started asking for help in turning their schools into more effective learning centers for students. That's a hill I'll climb, John. That's a mission I'll devote the rest of my career to."

"You're a good man, Dr. Evans."

"I've surrounded myself with good, talented people, John. People who are committed to making a difference and know how to do it. People who truly believe our schools can be run much more effectively. People like you, John. And building and developing that team has made all the difference."

* * *

In Blink, *Malcolm Gladwell (2005) explores the fascinating world of intuition, the subconscious, and knowing when something is right without having the detailed proof. Much too often, in education, we take the simple answer and turn it into a complicated maze of theory and stalling.*

SUMMARY

In an end-of-year conversation, John and the superintendent recognize how urgent the need is for our school principals of the twenty-first century to have gifted and caring mentors. And they embark on a plan to expand across the state the servant leadership model that has worked so well with Todd.

Chapter Twenty-Five

Closing Thoughts

To realize that our time on this Earth is but a few days, and understanding that those days will be best spent when serving others, is a bit of wisdom that makes all the difference. Decreasing, so others may increase—one of those paradoxical principles that can transform the fruits of any average life into a body of work that does indeed set the captives free.

Setting the captives free. I cannot think of a better phrase to describe what we educators do as our calling in life. Here is to all our principal colleagues, standing in the gap, leading their flock toward home.

IF I COULD GO BACK

- If I could be principal, for a little while longer, back at my old school, I'd bring flowers for my secretary often—because she was always there for me (and the entire school)—always.
- I would walk through the halls first thing in the mornings, and just stop and visit in classrooms and spend time with kids. After all, that's what I had set out to do, way back in college.
- I would have lunch with my teachers—all of them. Those who were hard to get along with, I'd tell them how much I appreciated their faithfulness. I had not walked in their shoes, so they sure didn't need

me "bossing." They needed me guiding, ever so gently, and modeling servant leadership—but with unconditional love and respect.
- I would throw an afterschool celebration for all of those volunteers who had given the school so much of themselves over the years.
- I would never again overpressure any staff person due to assessment. I would add back into the curriculum any classes that we had somehow started neglecting—health, foreign language, art, music, PE. Kids need all of these and more in truly being prepared for life during the few years we have them under our care.
- I'd hire a technology specialist (or two), regardless if the district agreed with me or not. And I'd turn this person loose in making our school a technology model for the region.
- I'd go out more at recess, and play kickball with the kids.
- I'd leave leadership meetings at central office if they went longer than two hours, if I had kids back in my building that day.
- I'd pay more attention in ARCs and not "doublespeak" to save the district some money.
- I'd not put anything in my teachers' mailboxes that was not urgent that week.
- I'd do away with most staff meetings (no more than once a month).
- I'd bring in advanced training on how to run effective teams, and then I'd empower my staff and parents to run these teams. I'd attend when I could, but I'd trust that they knew how to make good decisions that were about kids without me holding their hands.
- I'd add more recess and free time so the kids could enjoy the magic of their youth and not be worn out by February.
- I'd speak less and listen more. I'd apologize as often as I needed to.
- I'd post all key historical documents in hallways and on classroom walls, so as to not assist in sanitizing right out of our culture the ideals that made this culture!
- I'd provide training to all my staff on servant leadership and emotional intelligence.
- I'd refuse to ever in any form turn my head the other way while my school council got drawn into local political correctness. We'd go after the best teachers we could find, even if it took three months to find them. All teachers—every one—regardless of age, reputation, or experience, would have a mentor or instructional accountability

Closing Thoughts

team working with them (and I would have a mentor/accountability partner too).
- I'd meet regularly with a staff leadership team (separate from the school council team). These two teams would be provided extensive training on leadership research and what great schools look like.
- I'd go home at 4 a lot more often. I'd stay home more with my wife and kids on their sick days, or when it had snowed and my girls needed a good, old fashioned morning of sledding.
- I'd respect all others who tried to give me advice, and I'd listen, but I would not agree to anything that I knew my staff was not ready for.
- I'd give up some work days in the summer, taking that time to rest and renew, and to spend time with my family. And I'd take some time away from the office on fall break, Christmas break, and spring break.
- I'd exercise more, eat healthy, sleep more, and especially—take care of my spiritual needs and practice my faith habits first (which is critical). I'd not worry while at home about school—ever if I could help it. This would be my "emotional health" rule: At home, no thinking about school.
- I'd stay away from clerical work, and do less "busy" work at my desk, and instead be "out there" with my people several times during the school day.
- I would model instructional leadership by empowering and equipping every teacher and teacher's aide in the building—turning them loose as never before to do what they were trained to do. Yes, we all would be held accountable, with ongoing growth plans and professional development.
- I'd make sure we, the staff, were in control of the master schedule (instead of it controlling us), and would change it as often as needed.
- I would be relentless about reading, technology literacy, and math.
- I'd spend less money on copiers, and more money on student clubs, science lab and playground equipment, trade books for every classroom, and PE supplies. (And food for staff birthdays and other celebrations—every week if we had even half a good reason.)
- And I'd look at this list of 'people first' priorities, and hold my head high that I had indeed stayed true to my core values about serving others and running a school with utmost integrity, and then walk away—letting someone else have their turn.

- And as soon as I could, I'd get out in the woods, take a deep breath, and thank the good Lord for this walk I had been on all these years—this blessed walk with so many wonderful people and hundreds of precious children . . . this walk that was often lonely and stressful, but so fulfilling—all at the same time. And I'd simply say: "Thank You."

* * *

In Joy at Work, *Dennis Bakke (2005) shares how to revolutionize the local workplace by honoring and empowering employees and embracing their ideas on how to reinvent the organization.*

SUMMARY

This is my personal letter to the dedicated and talented staff I have supervised over the years. If I could go back, I would spend more of my time listening, supporting, coaching, and shepherding. Whatever each employee needed on that particular day, I would make sure I was there, both physically and emotionally. Most of the time I did practice this principle of "people first." But, "most of the time" should not be good enough. The best leaders are so little about themselves, and so much about their people, one does not even know they are in the building, but their influence is in every room.

References

Arbinger Institute. 2000. *Leadership and self-deception.* San Francisco: Berrett-Koehler.
Autry, J. A. 2001. *The servant leader.* New York: Crown Business.
Bakke, D. W. 2005. *Joy at work.* Seattle: UG.
Blanchard, K., and S. Johnson. 1981. *The one minute manager.* New York: William Morrow and Company, Inc.
Callahan, D. 2004. *The cheating culture.* Orlando: Harcourt, Inc.
Ciulla, J. B. 1998. *Ethics—The heart of leadership.* Westport, CT: Praeger Publishers.
Covey, S. R. 1989. *The 7 habits of highly effective people.* New York: Simon & Schuster.
DuFour, R., and R. Eaker. 1998. *Professional learning communities at work.* Bloomington, IN: National Testing Service.
Finzel, H. 1994. *The top ten mistakes leaders make.* Colorado Springs, CO: Cook Communications.
Fullan, M. 1997. *What's worth fighting for in the principalship?* New York: Teachers College Press.
Gladwell, M. 2005. *Blink.* New York: Little, Brown and Company.
Greenleaf, R. K. 1977. *Servant leadership—A journey into the nature of legitimate power and greatness.* Mahwah, NJ: Paulist Press.
Holcomb, E. L. 1996. *Asking the right questions.* Thousand Oaks, CA: Corwin Press, Inc.
Jensen, E. 1998. *Teaching with the brain in mind.* Alexandria, VA: Association for Supervision and Curriculum Development.
Keith, K. M. 2001. *Anyway.* New York: Berkley Books.

Marquardt, M. J., and N. O. Berger. 2000. *Global leaders for the 21st century.* Albany: State University of New York Press.

Maxwell, J. C. 2007. *Talent is never enough.* Nashville: Thomas Nelson.

McIntosh, G. L., and S. D. Rima, Sr. 1997. *Overcoming the dark side of leadership.* Grand Rapids, MI: Baker Books.

Rath, T. 2007. *Strengths finder 2.0.* New York: Gallup Press.

Rima, S. D. 2000. *Leading from the inside out.* Grand Rapids, MI: Baker Books.

Sanborn, M. 2002. *The fred factor.* Colorado Springs, CO: WaterBrook Press.

Senge, P. 2000. *Schools that learn.* New York: Doubleday.

Taylor, J., and W. Wacker. 2000. *The visionary's handbook—Nine paradoxes that will shape the future of your business.* New York: HarperBusiness.

Thorpe, R. 1995. *The first year as principal.* Portsmouth, NH: Heinemann.

Tichy, N. M., and M. A. Devanna. 1986. *The transformational leader.* New York: John Wiley & Sons, Inc.

About the Author

Rocky Wallace teaches graduate classes in instructional leadership for Morehead State University, and as a former principal, writes his articles and books from the unique perspective of the practitioner down in the trenches. While Wallace was principal at Catlettsburg Elementary in Boyd County, Kentucky, the school was named a Kentucky and U.S. Blue Ribbon School in 1996–1997. As he moved on to leadership consulting work with the Kentucky Department of Education in 2000, and later as Director of Instructional Support at the Kentucky Educational Development Corporation in Ashland, Kentucky, Wallace realized that school principals of this generation face a perplexing dilemma: They are being asked to do more and more in turning our nation's educational system around, and often by supervisors and others in leadership positions who have never sat in the principal's chair themselves.

While studying strategic leadership as he completed his doctoral work at Regent University, Wallace realized that the answer in how to create more effective schools that focus on the holistic needs of children and youth is in embracing the principles of servant leadership. Thus, the concept of "serving" and putting people over profit, while addressing key organizational culture issues, is found throughout his writing.

Wallace received his undergraduate degree from Berea College in 1979 and a MA from Morehead State in 1983. He has been married twenty-four years to Denise, who is the director of Calvary Christian School, located near Catlettsburg. The couple has two teenage daughters. Lauren is a student at Asbury College in Wilmore, Kentucky, and Bethany attends Calvary Christian with her mom.

In his spare time, Rocky pastors a small United Methodist church and also volunteers as a physical education teacher at Calvary. His hobbies include enjoying the outdoors and traveling with his family. He has authored several articles on instructional leadership, and wrote *Principal to Principal: Conversations in Servant Leadership and School Transformation*, published by Rowman and Littlefield Education in January 2008.

www.ingramcontent.com/pod-product-compliance
Lightning Source LLC
Chambersburg PA
CBHW031712230426
43668CB00006B/194